International Migration: A Very Short Introduction

VERY SHORT INTRODUCTIONS are for anyone wanting a stimulating and accessible way into a new subject. They are written by experts, and have been translated into more than 45 different languages.

The series began in 1995, and now covers a wide variety of topics in every discipline. The VSI library now contains over 500 volumes—a Very Short Introduction to everything from Psychology and Philosophy of Science to American History and Relativity—and continues to grow in every subject area.

Titles in the series include the following:

Khalid Koser

INTERNATIONAL MIGRATION

A Very Short Introduction

SECOND EDITION

OXFORD
UNIVERSITY PRESS

OXFORD

UNIVERSITY PRESS

Great Clarendon Street, Oxford, OX2 6DP,
United Kingdom

Oxford University Press is a department of the University of Oxford.
It furthers the University's objective of excellence in research, scholarship,
and education by publishing worldwide. Oxford is a registered trade mark of
Oxford University Press in the UK and in certain other countries

First edition published 2007
Second edition published 2016

Impression: 5

Published in the United States of America by Oxford University Press
198 Madison Avenue, New York, NY 10016, United States of America

British Library Cataloguing in Publication Data

Data available

Library of Congress Control Number: 2015960485

ISBN 978-0-19-875377-3

Printed in Great Britain by
Ashford Colour Press Ltd, Gosport, Hampshire

Contents

List of illustrations

The publisher and the author apologize for any errors or omissions in the above list. If contacted they will be pleased to rectify these at the earliest opportunity.

Abbreviations

CIS	Commonwealth of Independent States
EEA	European Economic Area
ELR	Exceptional Leave to Remain
EU	European Union
GCIM	Global Commission on International Migration
GDP	Gross Domestic Product
HDI	Human Development Index
HTA	Home Town Association
ICMPD	International Centre on Migration Policy Development
ICT	Inter-Corporate Transferee
IDP	Internally Displaced Person
ILO	International Labour Organization
IOM	International Organization for Migration
IPS	International Passenger Survey
LFS	Labour Force Survey
NAFTA	North American Free Trade Agreement
NGO	Non-Governmental Organization
NIC	Newly Industrializing Country
OECD	Organization for Economic Co-operation and Development
PRD	Pearl River Delta, China
SDGs	Sustainable Development Goals
UK	United Kingdom
UN	United Nations

UNDESA	United Nations Department of Economic and Social Affairs
UNDP	United Nations Development Program
UNHCR	Office of the United Nations High Commissioner for Refugees
USA	United States of America

Chapter 1
Why migration matters

Since the first edition of this book was published, international migration has only grown in relevance. The number of international migrants has increased by 20 per cent, and the number of irregular migrants by probably even more; while the number of refugees worldwide has doubled. Migrants are sending home more money than ever before, and their remittances are now recognized by the United Nations (UN) as one of the most important contributions to development and poverty reduction. While migrants continue to innovate and generate wealth in the countries where they settle, the challenges of integration have also become exacerbated. Migration has risen up the political agenda, in response to a growing incidence of humanitarian crises and disasters, but also as a result of a growing xenophobia and anti-immigrant sentiment in many countries. Migration has attracted particular attention in Australia and Europe in recent years, while remaining a global phenomenon.

This second edition has been updated in a number of ways. It includes the latest data on migration. It presents some of the most interesting and relevant new research on the issue. It focuses on new and topical case studies. And it covers recent global events such as the global financial crisis, the Arab Spring, the Syria conflict, the Ebola crisis, and the rise of ISIL, all of which have influenced migration patterns and processes.

The three underlying principles of the volume however remain constant, and their relevance has been heightened by the changes that have taken place over the last decade. First, it is important to try to inform debate on migration, by clarifying definitions and concepts and presenting current evidence. Who is a migrant? What is the difference between an asylum-seekers and a refugee? How do we count migrants? Are there too many migrants?

Second, a global perspective is essential. Most refugees in the world are in poorer countries. As many migrants move between countries of the South as from South to North. It is easy for those living in Europe or Australia to forget that other parts of the world currently face far greater migration influxes and challenges. The majority of migration is largely overlooked by the global media.

Third, a balanced perspective on migration is required. Approaches to migration have become more polarized, starker and more absolute. Generalizations abound. This volume, like the first edition, tries instead to strike an objective perspective. On the whole migration is positive; at times it has negative consequences. Most migrants want to work, some want to take advantage. In particular circumstances migrants may pose a risk, more often they represent potential. The lives and rights of migrants are usually more in jeopardy than the security of states; but not always.

A brief history of international migration

The history of migration begins with the origins of mankind in the Rift Valley in Africa, from where between about 1.5 million and 5000 BC *Homo erectus* and *Homo sapiens* spread initially into Europe and later into other continents. In the ancient world, Greek colonization and Roman expansion depended on migration, and outside Europe significant movements were also associated with the Mesopotamian, Inca, Indus, and Zhou empires. Other significant migrations in early history include that of the Vikings and of the Crusaders to the Holy Land.

In more recent history, it is possible to discern a series of major migration periods or events, according to migration historian Robin Cohen. Probably the predominant migration event in the 18th and 19th centuries was the forced transportation of slaves. An estimated 12 million people were forced from mainly western Africa to the New World, but also in lesser numbers across the Indian Ocean and Mediterranean. Besides its scale, one of the reasons this migration is so important is that it still resonates for descendants of slaves and among African Americans in particular. After the collapse of slavery, indentured labour from China, India, and Japan moved in significant numbers—some 1.5 million from India alone—to continue working the plantations of the European powers.

European expansion was also associated with large-scale voluntary resettlement from Europe, particularly to the colonies of settlement, the dominions, and the Americas. The great mercantile powers—Britain, the Netherlands, Spain, and France—all promoted settlement of their nationals abroad, not just of workers but also peasants, dissident soldiers, convicts, and orphans. Migration associated with expansion largely came to an end with the rise of anti-colonial movements towards the end of the 19th century, and indeed over the next fifty years or so there were some significant reverse flows back to Europe, for example, of the so-called *pieds noirs* to France.

The next period of migration was marked by the rise of the United States of America (USA) as an industrial power. Millions of workers from the stagnant economic regions and repressive political regimes of Northern, Southern, and Eastern Europe, not to mention those escaping the Irish famine, went to the USA from the 1850s until the Great Depression of the 1930s. Some

12 million of these migrants landed at Ellis Island in New York harbour for immigration inspections.

The next major period of migration was after the Second World War, when labour was needed to sustain booming post-war economies in Europe, North America, and Australia. This was the era when many Turkish migrants arrived to work in Germany and North Africans in France and Belgium, for example. It was also the period when about one million Britons migrated to Australia as so-called 'Ten Pound Poms'. During the same era decolonization was still having a migration impact in other parts of the world, most significantly in the movement of millions of Hindus and Muslims as a result of the Partition of India in 1947 and of Jews and Palestinians after the creation of Israel.

By the 1970s the international migrant labour boom was over in Europe, although it continued into the early 1990s in the USA. The engine-room of the global economy has begun to shift decisively to Asia, where labour migration is, in contrast, still growing. As we shall see later in this volume, the movement of asylum-seekers and refugees and irregular migrants has also become increasingly significant across the industrialized world in the last twenty years or so.

The purpose of this inevitably selective overview of international migration in recent history is not simply to make the point that migration is not a new phenomenon. It is also intended to signpost themes that will recur throughout this volume. That migration is associated with significant global events—revolutions, wars, and the rise and fall of empires; that it is associated with significant change—economic expansion, nation-building, and political transformations, and that it is also associated with significant problems—conflict, persecution, and dispossession. Migration has mattered through history, and continues to matter today.

Dimensions and dynamics of international migration

The United Nations (UN) defines as an international migrant a person who stays outside their usual country of residence for at least one year. According to that definition, the UN estimated that in 2013 there were about 232 million international migrants worldwide. This is roughly the equivalent of the fourth most populous country on earth, Indonesia. One in every thirty-five people in the world today is an international migrant.

Another way to put this is that only 3 per cent of the world's population today is an international migrant. But migration affects far more people than just those who migrate. It has important social, economic, and political impacts at home and abroad. According to Stephen Castles, Hein de Haas, and Mark Miller, authors of the influential book *The Age of Migration*:

> There can be few people in either industrialized or less developed countries today who do not have personal experience of migration and its effects; this universal experience has become the hallmark of the age of migration.

Between 1990 and 2013, the number of international migrants worldwide rose by 77 million, or 50 per cent. By 2013, some 135 million migrants lived in the developed world, and 95 million in the developing world. There were about 72 million migrants in Europe, 70 million in Asia, 53 million in North America, 18 million in Africa, and about 8 million in both Latin America and Australia. Almost 20 per cent of the world's migrants in 2000—about 46 million—lived in the USA (Figure 1). The Russian Federation was the second most important host country for migrants, with about 11 million, then Germany, Saudi Arabia, the UAE, and the UK with between 8–10 million migrants each.

1. The US–Mexico border is the most frequently crossed international border in the world—about 350 million people cross it each year.

It is much harder to say which countries most migrants come from, largely because origin countries do not keep count of how many of their nationals are living abroad. It has been estimated nevertheless that at least 35 million Chinese currently live outside their country, 20 million Indians, and 8 million Filipinos.

These facts and figures convey a striking message, and that is that international migration today affects every part of the world. Movements from 'South' to 'North' have increased as a proportion of total global migration; indeed, as is explained in Chapter 3, there are powerful reasons why people should leave poorer countries and head for richer ones (Figure 2). At the same time, it

2. A boat with migrants crossing the Mediterranean.

is important not to ignore the significant movements that still take place within regions. In 2013, the majority of migration occurred within—and not between—major areas. The majority of international migrants living in Africa (82 per cent) and Asia (76 per cent) were also born there. As shown in Chapter 6, there are far more refugees in the developing world than the developed world. Equally, more Europeans come to the UK each year, for example, than do people from outside Europe; and many of these Europeans are British citizens returning from stints overseas.

Besides the dimensions and changing geography of international migration, there are at least three trends that signify an important departure from earlier patterns and processes. First, the proportion of women among migrants has increased rapidly. Very nearly half the world's migrants were women in 2013. What is more, whereas women have traditionally migrated to join their partners abroad, an increasing proportion who migrate today do so independently; they are often the primary breadwinners for the families they leave behind.

7

There are a number of reasons why women comprise an increasing proportion of the world's migrants. One is that the demand for foreign labour, especially in more developed countries, is becoming increasingly gender-selective in favour of jobs typically fulfilled by women—services, healthcare, and entertainment. Second, an increasing number of countries have extended the right of family reunion to migrants—in other words allowing them to be joined by their spouses and children. Most often these spouses are women. Changing gender relations in some countries of origin also mean that women have more independence to migrate than previously. Finally, and especially in Asia, there has been a growth in the migration of women for domestic work (sometimes called the 'maid trade'); organized migration for marriage (sometimes referred to as 'mail order brides'); and the trafficking of women into the sex industry.

Another trend is the blurring of the traditional distinction between countries of origin, transit, and destination. Today almost every country in the world fulfils all three roles—migrants leave, pass through, and head for all of them. Perhaps no part of the world better illustrates this dynamic than the Mediterranean. About fifty years ago, all the countries of North Africa and Southern Europe were countries of origin for migrants who mainly went to Northern Europe to work. About twenty years ago Southern Europe changed from a region of emigration to a region of immigration, as increasing numbers of North Africans arrived to work in its growing economies and at the same time fewer Southern Europeans had an incentive to head north for work any more. At least until the Arab Spring, North Africa had also begun to transform from an origin to a transit and destination region, with the arrival of increasing numbers of migrants from sub-Saharan Africa. Most intend to cross the Mediterranean although large numbers remain in transit for long periods of time. Those who do enter Europe on the whole do so without authorization. Now North Africans are themselves fleeing the region, making North Africa simultaneously a region of origin, transit, and destination for migration.

Finally, while most of the major movements that took place over the last few centuries were permanent, today temporary migration has become much more important. Even people who have lived abroad for most of their lives often have a dream to return to the place of their birth, and it is now relatively unusual for people to migrate from one country to another and remain there for the rest of their lives. Furthermore, the traditional pattern of migrating once then returning home seems to be phasing out. An increasing number of people migrate several times during their lives, often to different countries or parts of the world, returning home in the intervening periods. Even those who are away for long periods of time return home at more and more frequent intervals, as international travel has become so much cheaper and more accessible.

Opportunities of international migration

Migration has been a constant and influential feature of human history. It has supported the growth of the world economy; contributed to the evolution of states and societies, and enriched many cultures and civilizations. Migrants have been amongst the most dynamic and entrepreneurial members of society: people who are prepared to take the risk of leaving their homes in order to create new opportunities for themselves and their children. The history of United States economic growth, for example, is in many ways the history of migrants: Andrew Carnegie (steel), Adolphus Busch (beer), Samuel Goldwyn (movies), and Helena Rubenstein (cosmetics) were all migrants. Kodak, Atlantic Records, RCA, NBC, Google, Intel, Hotmail, Sun Microsoft, Yahoo, and eBay were all started or co-founded by migrants.

In the contemporary world, international migration continues to play an important—although often unacknowledged—role in national, regional, and global affairs. In many developing countries, the money that migrants send home is a more important source of income than the official aid provided by richer countries. In certain developed countries, entire sectors of the economy and many public services have become highly dependent on migrant workers. It has been estimated by the World Bank that migrant labour around the world earns US$20 trillion—the vast majority of which is invested in the countries where they work. A recent study indicated that European migrants in the United Kingdom (UK) between 2000 and 2011 added over £20 billion to public finances.

Migrants and migration do not just contribute to economic growth; in fact their impact is probably most keenly felt in the social and cultural spheres of life. Throughout the world, people of different national origins, who speak different languages, and who have different customs, religions, and ways of living are coming into unprecedented contact with each other. Whether they are willing to admit it or not, most societies today are characterized by at least a degree of diversity. In the last 24 hours you have almost certainly eaten food or listened to music originating elsewhere in the world, or watched a top-flight sports team that includes foreign-born players. It is no coincidence that some of the largest concentrations of migrants are to be found in 'global cities' like Hong Kong, London, or New York: dynamic, innovative and highly cosmopolitan urban centres that enable people, places, and cultures in different parts of the world to become increasingly interconnected.

Challenges of international migration

It would be naïve, at the same time, to deny that international migration today also poses important challenges. Perhaps the most talked about is the linkage between migration and security. Especially after 9/11 there has been a perception of a close connection between international migration and terrorism. This has been compounded more recently by the radicalization of some migrants, and the new phenomenon of 'foreign terrorist fighters'. Irregular migration, which is increasing, is sometimes regarded by politicians and the public alike as a threat to national sovereignty and public security. In a number of destination countries, host societies have become increasingly fearful about the presence of migrant communities, especially those with unfamiliar cultures that come from parts of the world associated with extremism and violence.

These are legitimate concerns that should not be underestimated; they are examined in greater depth in Chapters 2–8. At the same time, there has probably been too much attention paid to the challenges posed by migration for destination countries and societies in which migrants settle; and not enough to those that arise for the migrants themselves, their families, as well as for the people and societies they leave behind.

It is worth remembering, for a start, that many migrants leave their homes because they have no choice. Today there are almost 20 million refugees worldwide—these are people who have been forced to flee their homes for fear of persecution or death. Once their journey has begun, many migrants (and not just refugees) perish en route. In 2015 thousands have died trying to cross the Mediterranean. Some migrants, furthermore, find themselves exploited and their human rights abused once they have arrived at their destination. This is most particularly true for the victims of human trafficking who can effectively be enslaved, often in the sex industry. Domestic workers, too, can face abuse and suffer violence at the hands of their employers. More generally, many migrants and their children face discrimination and prejudice, even years after they have settled abroad. Migration matters just as much because of its negative consequences for migrants themselves as it does for the challenges it poses for destination societies.

Migration also can have important implications for the societies migrants leave. As I explain in Chapter 4, this is especially the case where migrants have skills that are in short supply in their home countries. While the impact of the so-called 'brain drain' has been felt most severely in the health sector, it is significant in the education sector too. Not only does it reduce the ability of poor countries to deliver essential services, it also means that public investment in the education and training of these people is effectively lost to the country.

A very short introduction to international migration

For the sorts of reasons outlined in this chapter, international migration is right at the top of political agendas in many countries, attracts considerable media coverage, and has become a common topic of public interest more generally. Yet all too often the debate on migration is unsatisfactory. Concepts are unclear. Statistics are at times quoted in ways that alarm rather than inform. Only a very partial picture of migration is normally presented. Overall, the real diversity and complexity of migration is often ignored.

Against this background, the intention of this *Very Short Introduction* is to try to provide the reader with the explanations, analysis, and data required to understand today's key migration issues, and hopefully to engage in reasonable debate. As someone who has taught and researched migration and related issues for over twenty years, I naturally have my own perspectives and opinions. But I have tried to keep these in the background, in order to present a full picture of the debates that surround migration today. Equally, this book is not centrally concerned with migration policy, but where relevant some commentary on policy implications is included.

To try to condense any large field of research, writing, and political argument into such a short book inevitably requires selectivity, and different authors would make different choices faced with this challenge. It is initially worth emphasizing that, as the book's title indicates, its focus is migration across borders. The main reasons are that international migration has been the subject of far more research and writing than internal migration, and has also attracted far more political and media attention and public discourse. At the same time, it has to be acknowledged that there are far more internal migrants than international migrants.

I have tried to make use of 'real life' examples that are taken from my own research—this is one way to try to gain a perspective on the experiences of migrants themselves. To supplement my own limited knowledge, I have also referred to the published findings of research by scholars in the field. I have structured the book around what I view as the most topical and relevant issues in international migration today, rather, for example, than writing a chapter on migration in each of the world's main regions. Coverage of each of these issues is necessarily concise, and so at the end of the book I refer the reader to other sources to which they can turn for more detailed information and analysis.

Chapter 2
Who is a migrant?

Ostensibly the answer to the question 'Who is a migrant?' is straightforward: most countries have adopted the UN definition of someone living outside their own country for a year or more. In reality, however, the answer is more complicated. First, the concept 'migrant' covers a wide range of people in a wide variety of situations. Second, it is very hard to count migrants and to determine how long they have been abroad. Third, just as important as defining when a person becomes a migrant is to define when they stop being a migrant. One way for this to happen is to return home; another is to become a citizen of a new country, and the procedures governing that transformation vary significantly. Finally, it has been suggested that, as a result of globalization, there are now new 'types' of migrants with new characteristics, for example comprising transnational communities or diasporas.

Migrant categories

There are three main ways that international migrants are normally categorized. A common distinction, first of all, is between 'voluntary' and 'forced' migrants. The latter are people who have been forced to leave their own country, because of conflict, persecution, or for environmental reasons such as drought or famine. These people are usually described as refugees, although as is shown in Chapter 6 in fact the term refugee has a very specific meaning, and does not include all forced migrants.

A related second distinction that is often made is between people who move for political reasons and those who move for economic reasons. The former are usually refugees—people who have been obliged to leave because of political persecution or conflict. The latter are usually described as labour migrants—in other words people who move to find work, or better job opportunities and working conditions. They in turn are often further classified as low skilled or highly skilled (see Box 1). Somewhere in between economic and political migrants there are also people who move primarily for what might be considered social reasons. Most commonly these are women and children who are moving to join their husbands, who have found work abroad, through the process of family reunion. There are other examples of social migration, such as where people move for love or marriage. The final main distinction is between legal and 'illegal' migrants—although the

Box 1 Highly skilled migrants

A growing proportion of people who move for largely economic reasons are now classified as highly skilled migrants. Often their movement is facilitated by selective visa systems that allocate points according to the education and qualifications of the applicant. A particular type of highly skilled migrant is inter-corporate transferees (ICTs)—that is, people who move internationally but within the same firm. Worldwide there is a significant international movement of students too, and they often are also included in the category of highly skilled migrants. There is increasing competition between states for the limited supply of highly skilled migrants worldwide, mainly because of the disproportionate effect they have on economic growth through innovation and expertise.

term 'irregular' is possibly more accurate and probably less derogatory than 'illegal' when talking of migrants (see Chapter 5). The concept 'irregular' migrants covers a wide range of people, principally migrants who enter a country either without documents or with forged documents, or migrants who enter legally but then stay after their visa or work permit has expired. It is more or less impossible to enumerate accurately irregular migrants worldwide, but what is sure is that there are far more legal migrants than irregular migrants.

Categorizations always simplify reality, and this is true of these migration categories in at least three ways. First, there is some overlap between the different categorizations. Thus most voluntary migrants are also economic migrants, and many forced migrants are political migrants or refugees.

Second, the sharp distinctions drawn between migrants within each categorization are often more blurred in reality. Very few migrations, for example, are purely voluntary or involuntary. Many large corporations, for instance, consider moving staff between international offices to be part of their training. So whilst employees are ostensibly moving voluntarily, they may have no option if they want to keep their job with that firm. At the other end of the spectrum, even refugees have choices other than to leave their own country. They could stay and take a risk, or move to a neighbouring village or town, or take sides in the conflict.

The same blurring applies to distinctions between economic and political migration. Consider the case of someone who leaves their home because they lose their job. On the face of it they are moving for economic reasons. But what if they have lost their job because of their race or religion or gender? In that case it might be argued that they are fleeing for political reasons. The analytical challenge here is to distinguish between underlying causes of migration and its immediate precipitants.

Third, and a related point, is that individuals can effectively 'transform' from one type of migrant to another within the various categorizations. A legal migrant may overstay his or her work permit and thus become classified as an irregular migrant. Or an individual might leave his or her country voluntarily but then not be able to return, as a result of the start of a war or a change of government, and thus effectively become an involuntary migrant, forced to stay outside their own country.

What do the statistics mean?

Another reason it is so hard to answer the question 'who is a migrant' is because it is difficult to count migrants. Let us focus for a few paragraphs on the case of the UK to illustrate this, whilst also recognizing that different countries have very different methods for counting migrants.

There are three very important observations to make about statistics on migration in the UK. First, even official migration statistics cannot provide a complete picture of international migration in the UK. To put this rather more bluntly, even the government cannot state with any confidence how many people enter or leave the country each year. The most obvious reason is that official migration statistics do not include irregular migrants. Statistics on irregular migrants in the UK are no more than guesses. Chapter 5 looks at statistics on irregular migration in more detail.

Second, there are important reservations surrounding the statistics on migration that the government does record. Most published statistics on migration into and out of the UK are based on the International Passenger Survey (IPS). This is a small sample survey conducted at seaports and airports. Passengers are interviewed about their intentions of staying in the UK (or staying abroad, if leaving). Those who intend to stay in or out of the UK for a year or more are counted as migrants. One problem is coverage: only a tiny fraction of the population is interviewed and the results are scaled up. Another is that people's intentions often change—they may or may not stay or stay away as long as they intended. Adjustments are made to the IPS figures to try to take account of such problems.

There are two other main sources of data on migration flows in the UK. Work permits issued measure the entry of workers, but only from outside the European Economic Area (EEA) because work permits are not required by citizens of EEA member states. Asylum statistics show how many people apply for protection in the UK, but great care is required in interpreting them, as sometimes they include dependants (spouses and children) and sometimes not. Alternative indicators of numbers of migrants entering the UK include the Labour Force Survey (LFS), which records nationality and address one year ago, but again is based only on a sample of households. The national census also records address a year ago, but it does not record nationality, and it takes place only once every decade.

If these sorts of problems are found in the UK, a small island and one of the most advanced economies in the world, imagine how difficult it is to count migrants elsewhere: in poor countries that do not have the necessary skills or expertise or capacity to monitor their borders; in countries with long land borders, or in places where sudden large-scale movements take place across borders.

Return migration

Returning home is one way that people stop being migrants— although often even after returning home people maintain elements of new practices and identities they have developed abroad. There are no global estimates on the scale of return migration, although most experts believe that it is substantial.

Data on return migration share many of the problems that characterize data on international migration more generally.

A particular problem is that the measurement of return migration has traditionally not been a priority in either countries of origin or in host countries, as for neither set of countries has it generally been considered a problem in the same way that the emigration of nationals and immigration of non-nationals often have. Even where host and origin countries do purport to have recorded the same return flow, there can be significant differences in their estimations. A good example cited in a ground-breaking article on return migration by Russell King is that during the 1970s German data on Italian repatriation exceeded Italian statistics on return migration from Germany by a factor of at least two. Part of the reason for this sort of inconsistency can be gleaned from a more recent example from Poland, where return migration during the 1990s was substantial but remained uncounted in official statistics, simply because most Polish emigrants during the 1980s left without registering as emigrants. Similarly, in Turkey there are no institutions which record data in relation to the emigration or return of migrant workers—estimates on return rely only on data collected in host countries.

From migrants to citizens

Another way migration ends is through migrants becoming citizens in a new country. In some countries this is a relatively easy and quick process; in others it is virtually impossible for all but a select few. The explanation for this variation is less to do with the characteristics of the migrants themselves than with the histories, ideologies, and structures of the states involved.

Laws on citizenship and nationality derive from two alternative principles. One is *ius sanguinis* (law of the blood), according to which in order to become a citizen one needs to be descended from a national of the country in question. The alternative principle is *ius soli* (law of the soil), which is based on birth in the territory of the country.

In practice, all modern states have citizenship rules based on a combination of these two principles (Israel is an exception), although one or the other tends to be predominant (Table 1). Germany, for example, broadly followed the principle of *ius sanguinis* until a change of policy in 2000. This explains why even the children and grandchildren of post-war immigrants from Turkey, who were born and raised in Germany, have traditionally been excluded from German citizenship. It equally explains why, during the reunification of Germany, people whose families had lived outside Germany for a number of generations, mainly in Eastern Europe or the former Soviet Union, were automatically granted German citizenship. In contrast, Australia, Canada, the UK, and the USA, for example, broadly follow the principle of *ius*

Table 1 Citizenship rules in selected countries

Country	Principle underlying citizenship	Period of residence for naturalization	Whether dual nationality allowed
Australia	Combination	3 years	Yes
Austria	*Ius sanguinis*	10 years	No
Belgium	Combination	5 years	Yes
Canada	*Ius soli*	3 years	Yes
France	*Ius sanguinis*	5 years	Yes
Germany	*Ius sanguinis* (until 2000)	8 years	No
Israel	Open to any resident Jew	0	Yes
Netherlands	*Ius sanguinis*	5 years	Yes
Sweden	*Ius sanguinis*	5 years	No
UK	Combination	5 years	Yes
USA	*Ius soli*	5 years	Yes

soli, so that any child born to a legal immigrant in that country is automatically entitled to citizenship there.

Whatever the underlying principle for acquiring citizenship, most countries also permit migrants to become naturalized after being legally resident for a certain number of years: the *ius domicili* principle. The number of years varies widely, from just three years in Australia and Canada to ten years in Austria and Germany.

Not only do the rules governing acquisition of citizenship vary between countries, so too do the criteria of citizenship. Some countries, for example, permit dual nationality, and thus do not insist that an immigrant abandons his or her original nationality in order to become a citizen of the new country; in others this is not the case. As we see in the section on 'Migrants, diasporas, and transnational communities', the growth of dual and even triple nationality is one reason for the emergence of transnationalism among some migrant communities.

In addition, in some countries, full citizenship can only be acquired at the price of cultural assimilation, while other countries enable new citizens to maintain their distinct cultural identities. These outcomes arise from two competing models of integration. Assimilation is one model, which is a one-sided process whereby migrants are expected to give up their distinctive linguistic, cultural, and social characteristics and become indistinguishable from the majority population. Broadly France follows this model. The main alternative is multiculturalism which refers to the development of immigrant populations into ethnic communities that remain distinguishable from the majority population with regard to language, culture, and social behaviour. Australia, Canada, the Netherlands, the UK, and the USA all follow variations on this model.

There is of course a difference between laws and policies on integration, and the actual experiences of the people involved.

Integration can be defined simply as the process by which immigrants become accepted into society, both as individuals and groups. The Global Commission on International Migration considered integration to be 'a long-term and multi-dimensional process, requiring a commitment on the part of both migrants and non-migrant members of society to respect and adapt to each other, thereby enabling them to interact in a positive and peaceful manner'.

Migrants, diasporas, and transnational communities

Arguably just as important as how formal structures or host societies define who is and is not a migrant is the sense of identity of migrants themselves. There has been a plethora of writing on this topic in the last few years, focusing in particular on two concepts: transnationalism and diasporas. Both concepts are complex and contested, and are defined here in as simple terms as possible.

The term diaspora has classical connotations and has normally been used to refer to the exodus of the Jews following the destruction of the Second Temple in AD 70. Until its recent revival the concept was also at times applied to African slaves and to Armenians who fled the massacre perpetrated by the Ottoman Empire during and immediately after the First World War. What these experiences have in common are large-scale involuntary displacements and an inability to return home, coupled with a great yearning to do so.

To varying degrees these characteristics have been identified in more recent movements, and there has been a resurgence in the usage of the concept of diaspora (see Box 2). According to theorist Gabriel Sheffer in *Modern Diasporas in International Politics*: 'Modern diasporas are ethnic minority groups of migrant origins residing and acting in host countries but maintaining strong

Box 2 'New' African diasporas

Given that African slaves comprised one of the few groups to which the concept diaspora was traditionally applied, it is interesting that it is now being adopted by more recent African migrants to describe themselves and their organizations. During research among various African communities in London, one question I asked was why they were using the term. Three reasons emerged. One was the perception on the part of these communities that there are fewer negative connotations currently associated with the term diaspora than with the terms 'immigrant', 'refugee', or 'asylum-seeker'. Perhaps as a result of its long-standing association with the dispersal of Jews and African slaves, the term has yet to be adopted in a derogatory manner. Second, for at least some communities the term appears to be 'self-motivational'. Diaspora is becoming a 'buzzword' rather like globalization, and for some communities it appears to have connotations with which they are keen to be associated. Finally, for at least some communities, there is a sense that their experiences in some way compare with those of the original diasporas—that they too are victims, just as were dispersed Jews and African slaves.

sentimental and material links with their countries of origin—their home lands'.

A related concept is that of 'transnational communities'. In very simple terms, the idea is that some migrants have begun to live 'in between' nations. They maintain sustained social, economic, and political contacts with people and places in their country of origin that transcend national boundaries. According to leading migration scholar Alejandro Portes, writing in *International Migration Review*, transnational communities comprise dense networks across political borders created by immigrants in their quest for economic advancement and social recognition. Through these networks, an increasing number of people are able to live dual lives. Participants are often bilingual, move easily between cultures, frequently maintain homes in two countries, and pursue economic, political and cultural interests that require their presence in both.

By implication, these people are beginning to escape the confines of political definitions such as immigrant or citizen. In *Migration in Asia-Pacific* (ed. R. Iredale et al.), Stephen Castles considers the implications for citizenship of transnationalism as follows:

> Transnationalism will inevitably lead to a rapid rise in multiple citizenship—creating the phenomenon most feared by nationalists—the potentially divided loyalties of people with an instrumental rather than emotional attitude toward state membership. The growth of transnationalism may in the long run lead to a rethinking of the very contents of citizenship.

Chapter 3
Migration and globalization

The concept of globalization is complex and contested. David Held, a leading theorist of globalization, in his book *Global Transformations*, has provided the following definition: 'Globalization may be thought of as a process (or set of processes) which embodies a transformation in the spatial organization of social relations and transactions—assessed in terms of their extensity, intensity, velocity and impact—generating transcontinental or inter-regional flows and networks of activity, interaction, and the exercise of power.' These processes have already resulted in an increase in the goods, ideas, information, and capital flowing across borders and many commentators argue that globalization is also increasing the flow of people across borders too.

International migration is an important dimension of globalization, and has become increasingly embedded in changes in global economic and social structures. Growing developmental, demographic, and democratic disparities provide powerful incentives to move, as does the global jobs crisis affecting large parts of the developing world. The segmentation of labour markets in richer countries is creating increasing demand for migrant workers there. A revolution in communications has facilitated growing awareness of disparities and opportunities for would-be migrants, while transformations in transportation have made mobility cheaper and more readily accessible. Migration networks have expanded rapidly and further facilitate migration. New individual rights and entitlements allow certain people to cross borders and stay abroad more easily. And the growth of a migration industry adds further momentum to international migration, even where it is not officially permitted. In sum, this chapter shows why there are more reasons and additional means to migrate than ever before.

Growing disparities

According to the United Nations Development Program (UNDP) in 2013 2.2 billion people—or 15 per cent of the world's population—were poor. 842 million—12 per cent—suffered from chronic hunger. More than one billion people lacked access to safe water and 2.6 billion did not have adequate sanitation. Worldwide about 115 million children were denied even basic primary education—most of them in sub-Saharan Africa and South Asia. On average girls could expect to receive one year less of education than boys in African and Arab states and two years less in South Asia. In the developing world as a whole, only 58 per cent of women were literate, compared with 68 per cent of men.

A lack of development is compounded by growing population pressure. Almost 5 billion people, or 80 per cent of the world's population, currently live in poor or at best middle-income countries. While many of the world's more prosperous countries have declining populations, they are burgeoning in many poorer countries: virtually all of the world's population growth currently takes place in developing nations. The average woman in Africa today has 5.2 children while the average European woman has just 1.4. These trends mean that the share of the world's residents in developing countries will rise even further. And as a result of such high rates of childbirth in the developing world, there is also a far higher proportion of younger people there than in the developed world.

It is no coincidence that a good number of poor countries are also states where the democratic process is fragile, where the rule of law is weak, and where corruption is rife. By migrating, people try to protect themselves and their families against the effects of a weak economy and volatile markets, and from political crises, armed conflicts, and other risks. In some cases, people are forced to flee as refugees, as the state can no longer protect them from the impact of conflict or from persecution. In the very worst cases, it is the states themselves that are responsible for these offences.

But it is important to stress that it is not necessarily underdevelopment or overpopulation or poor governance per se that cause migration, but rather differentials between different parts of the world. Per capita Gross Domestic Product (GDP), which is the most commonly used economic indicator for what people earn, is sixty-six times higher in the developed world than in the developing world. A child born in Burkina Faso today can expect to live thirty-five fewer years than a child born in Japan; and somebody born in India can expect to live fourteen fewer years than somebody born in the United States. Limited school enrolment and low literacy levels in poorer countries compare with almost universal enrolment and full literacy in the richer ones. And with very few exceptions the most corrupt and undemocratic governments are in the poorest countries.

The global jobs crisis

One of the most powerful incentives to migrate is to find work. Although it spiked during the global financial crisis between 2008 and 2010, overall unemployment has declined in the developed world in recent decades. In contrast it has increased or remained at a stable but high level in most of the developing world. The highest incidence of unemployment in the world's major regions is in the Middle East and North Africa at over 12 per cent, compared with about 6 per cent across the industrialized economies.

Being out of work is not the only dimension of the global jobs crisis. Many people are underemployed. Usually they work in the informal sector, where employment is unpredictable; opportunities come and go by the season and in some cases by the week or even day, and working conditions can be appalling. Even for those who are employed, wages are often barely sufficient for survival. UNDP estimates that, although poverty is likely to decrease, it will still remain substantial for the foreseeable future and that in 2015 some 380 million people are still trying to survive on less than one US dollar per day. Another aspect of the global jobs crisis is the 12 million people estimated by the International Labour Organization (ILO) to be currently working in situations of forced labour.

A population that is under particular stress in the developing world relies on agriculture for their income. They comprise about half of the entire labour force—some 1.3 billion people. Many have small farms that are threatened by commercial expansion and environmental degradation. They are also often taxed disproportionately because of their weak political position. The income gap between farming and non-farming activities in developing countries has increased dramatically in recent years. One result has been increasing rural–urban migration, as farmers and their families head for towns and cities to try to find a better source of livelihood. For many of these people, internal migration to the city is the first step towards international migration out of their country.

The segmentation of labour markets

High-income economies are increasingly becoming characterized by the segmentation of labour markets. This occurs where sectors of the labour market are rejected by native workers because they are low-paying, have little security, and are low status, and thus have become dominated by migrant workers. These are often described as '3D jobs'—entailing work that is dirty, dangerous,

3. Undocumented migrant farm workers in North Carolina, USA.

or difficult, and often a combination. They are concentrated in sectors such as agriculture, timber, plantations, heavy industry, construction, and domestic service (Figure 3). Even during the global financial crisis native workers were reluctant to work in these jobs, and so demand for migrant workers continued to some extent irrespective of economic trends.

Often the migrants who work in these sectors are undocumented or have irregular status, for they more than others are willing to work for very low wages and in insecure conditions. In the USA it is often irregular Mexican migrants who work the farms, in the Russian Federation irregular migrants keep heavy industry working, and in the UK and several other European countries construction, the food industry, and many services rely on irregular migrants. If your pizza last night was cheap, it may well be because the people working in the kitchen have irregular status and are therefore earning less than the minimum wage. The advantage for employers is that irregular migrants are flexible and inexpensive. The migrants themselves, however, are often exploited and abused.

The communications and transportation revolutions

The communications revolution is a central element of the globalization process. Much of the academic literature on globalization has focused on the recent explosion in hi-tech developments such as email and the internet, electronic bulletin boards and satellite television stations, as well as cell phones and cheap international telephone calls (see Box 3). It has been estimated, for example, that between 1990 and 2015 the number of internet users increased from scarcely one million to over three billion. This revolution has facilitated increasing global linkages and, in effect, reduced the distance between different parts of the world. It is relevant to migration for two reasons. First, it makes people aware of disparities, of what life is like in other parts of the world. Second, it makes people aware of opportunities to move

Box 3 The cell phone revolution in Africa

It is estimated that just over half the world's population now use cell phones. The majority are based in developing countries, making cell phones the first telecommunications technology in history to have more users there than in the developed world. Cell phone usage in Africa is growing faster than in any other region, where it has been estimated that cell phone usage will increase 20 fold in the next ten years—double the rate of growth in the rest of the world.

4. Homeless man sitting next to an internet café in Bangalore, India.

and to work abroad. As is indicated in Chapter 8, technology is
likely to be one of the most important influences on the future
of migration.

At the same time it is possible to overstate the communications
revolution (Figure 4). There is still a significant global 'digital
divide', which is the term given to the gap in access to information

resources that exists between poor and rich countries. This was most strikingly illustrated in a speech by the UN Secretary-General Kofi Annan in 2000, when he said that 'Half the world's population has never made or received a phone call', although this statistic has been widely debated ever since. Bridging the digital divide is nevertheless considered important for achieving global equality, increasing social mobility, encouraging democracy, and promoting economic growth.

Another 'revolution' often referred to in the globalization literature is in transportation. This refers, on the one hand, to the increasing range of options for international travel and, on the other, to decreasing costs. It has particularly arisen because of the proliferation of competition between airline companies. Once again it would be a mistake to assume that this revolution has reached every part of the world, but it is nevertheless estimated that today it costs no more than US$2,500 to travel legally between any two places in the world. As is shown in Chapter 5, it can be far more expensive—but is still possible—to travel illegally. If the communications revolution has made many would-be migrants more aware of reasons to migrate, the transportation revolution has made migration more feasible. Once again, however, it is important not to overestimate its impact: travelling internationally is still prohibitively expensive for the majority of the world's population, and many face administrative obstacles such as obtaining passports and visas.

Migration networks

Most migrants move to countries where they have friends or family already established, forming what are often referred to as transnational migration networks. It has been argued that one of the main reasons why migration is increasing today is these migration networks, which establish a self-perpetuating cycle. The expansion of migration means that more people than ever before have friends or family already living abroad, and the changing geography of migration means that more often than previously these networks link would-be migrants in poor countries with potential destinations in richer countries.

Migration networks have been shown to encourage migration in three main ways. First, they provide information, often taking advantage of new communications technology. Second, they finance trips by lending would-be migrants money. Third, they have also been shown to play a crucial role in helping new migrants to settle, by providing an initial place to stay, helping them find a job, and providing other economic and social assistance.

Research has demonstrated that the character of migration networks varies considerably depending on local histories of migration, national conditions, and socio-cultural traits of the migrants involved. An important general observation about migration networks, nevertheless, is that they continue to operate largely regardless of the level of economic prosperity in destination countries. Research also indicates that it is difficult for policy to disrupt the momentum associated with migration networks.

New rights and entitlements

There has been a significant expansion of rights and entitlements that allow certain people to cross borders and stay abroad far more easily than ever before. The dismantling of internal borders in the European Union (EU), for example, allows for the free movement of EU citizens within the region, while the North American Free Trade Agreement (NAFTA) and regional economic agreements in other parts of the world, including Africa and South America, also contain some provisions for the free movement of workers. Furthermore, certain categories of people—such as businesspeople, academics and students, sports and entertainment performers—often either do not require visas or can apply via fast-track procedures. More countries than ever before also allow long-term migrant workers to be joined by members of their immediate family. And towards the other end of the migration spectrum, most countries in the world have signed the 1951 UN Refugee Convention which guarantees protection and assistance to refugees outside their country (see Chapter 6).

The extent of these new rights and entitlements can, however, be exaggerated. The free movement of labour has not yet been realized in most regional economic agreements outside the EU. In the USA security concerns have impacted on immigration policies to the extent that the number of H1-B visas issued to specialist and expert immigrants has more than halved since 9/11. Applicants for family reunion face increasingly rigorous administrative processes. There are also increasing restrictions on the mobility of many other people—the low-skilled and asylum-seekers, for example.

The migration industry

Migration has always generated business (see Box 4). Today it is facilitated by a wide range of individuals and agents including

Box 4 The migration industry in historical perspective

The migration industry is not new, although its scale and profit are new characteristics. Writing in 1977 about emigration from Italy to the USA at the end of the 19th century, historian Robert Harney coined the term 'the commerce of migration' when he wrote that: 'It is clear that bureaucrat, notary, lawyer, innkeeper, loan shark, mercante di campagna, runners in the harbour city, agents, even train conductors depended on the emigration trade.' Jorge Durand also described the prominent role played by recruiters in encouraging migration from central western Mexico to the USA at the end of the 19th century by connecting the workforces of that region with industries that needed their labour in the American south-west.

labour recruiters, immigration lawyers, travel agents, brokers, housing providers, remittances agencies, immigration and customs officials, as well as by entire institutions such as the International Organization for Migration (IOM), which is often responsible for transporting migrants and refugees for official resettlement or return programmes, and NGOs that provide assistance and shelter to migrants and refugees. These have been described by some analysts as forming a new migration 'industry' or migration 'business', that just like any other business stands to make a commercial gain. As is explained in Chapter 5 there is also an illegitimate part of the migration industry, comprising human traffickers and migrant smugglers.

The enormous profits that the immigration industry makes from migration, it has been argued, add considerable momentum to the process. At the same time its increasing complexity—linking highly organized groups with small operators and subagents in origin, transit, and destination countries—makes it difficult for policy to intervene to reduce its impact.

Explaining migration

This chapter has briefly explained some of the key structural changes in the global economy that together provide increasing incentives and opportunities for people to migrate. Yet these need to be reconciled with the fact that still only about 3 per cent of the world's population is an international migrant. Given growing inequalities, widening awareness of opportunities for a better life elsewhere, and increasing access to transportation, a legitimate question to ask is, why do so few people migrate?

Some of the answers to this question have already been alluded to. The very poorest people, those most affected by global inequalities, simply cannot afford to move. Many people who do migrate in response to poverty move internally, normally from the countryside to the city, and not internationally. There are far more unemployed or underemployed people in the poor world than jobs for them even in the segmented labour markets of the rich economies. The communications and transportation revolutions are not as far-reaching as some commentators believe, nor are migration networks. Rights and entitlements to move on the whole apply to the privileged few. And the migration industry depends on profit and so has an incentive to keep migration costs up.

At least three other reasons emerge from the literature. The most important is inertia. Most people do not want to move away from family, friends, and a familiar culture, so most people stay in the country where they were born. Another reason is that governments can control migration. Communist countries used to stop people leaving, but since the collapse of the Soviet Union and end of the cold war this is rarely the case any more (Cuba and North Korea are notable exceptions). Much more common today are destination countries controlling migration—although their efforts are not always effective. An additional reason is that, as countries develop, emigration eventually reduces, and despite the depressing statistics outlined earlier in this chapter ('Growing disparities'), most countries in the world are developing, albeit at times at a painfully slow rate. The links between migration and development are examined in Chapter 4.

Chapter 4
Migration and development

International migration is related to development in two main ways. Chapter 3 considered one, namely how disparities in development can be an incentive to migrate. This chapter considers the relationship in reverse, asking how international migration impacts on development in origin countries. On the positive side, migrants send home vast sums of money and make other contributions from abroad too, and when they return they can bring home new skills, experiences, and contacts. On the negative side, and as already alluded to in Chapter 1, migration can deplete countries of skills that are in short supply through the 'brain drain'.

Remittances

The term remittance usually refers to money sent home by migrants abroad. As I hope has become clear by now, almost everything related to migration is difficult to quantify accurately, and this is certainly true of remittances. While some money is sent home through banking systems and thus can be formally tracked, it is likely that more is sent home through informal channels. One reason is the high costs that are often charged by banks and agents—the global average in 2015 is 8 per cent. Channels for informal remittances include migrants taking home cash when they return for visits, or sending home money with

5. Billboard advertising an international money transfer company in Mogadishu, Somalia.

friends or relatives. Sometimes entrepreneurs and traders who travel regularly to and from home carry money back for migrants for a small commission—in Cuba, for example, these entrepreneurs are known as *mulas*. Perhaps the most elaborate mechanism for informal transfers, however, is the Somali *hawilaad* system (Figure 5). The point is that the scale of these informal transfers is simply not known. Furthermore, even formal remittances cannot always be accurately quantified, as banks are often unwilling or unable to release specific details about personal transfers.

These data problems notwithstanding, the World Bank produces annual estimates of the scale of remittances worldwide. They estimate that in 2015 some US\$586 billion was sent home by migrants. This is a quite staggering sum. According to some analysts, in terms of value formal remittances now represent the second largest transfer of any legal commodity (thus excluding narcotics) worldwide, after oil. In developing countries remittances are the most important source of external funding after corporate investments, and they amount to almost double the value of donations through development assistance and charity.

The rate of growth of remittances around the world is also remarkable—the 2015 total is more than three times the total reported in the first edition of this book, in 2007. The main reason remittances have increased so rapidly in recent years is the globalization process. Specifically, there are '3Ts' that have been generated by globalization and, at the same time, promote remittances. One is transportation—particularly cheap air transportation. The second is the growth in tourism—many migrants carry home money when they visit for a holiday. The third is telecommunications—cheap telephone calls and widening internet access mean that migrants and their families can stay in contact more regularly than previously, and friends and families can request assistance more easily. It is now also increasingly common to transfer money using cell phones, although more traditional methods like the *hawilaad* system are still significant (see Box 5).

Box 5 The *hawilaad* system

The *hawilaad* (or *xawilaad*) system is mainly based on Somali traders. They collect hard currency from Somali migrants abroad then use the money to purchase commodities that can be sold in Somalia. They return periodically to Somalia, sell their goods, then pay the equivalent in Somali currency to the migrants' families. Profit made on the sale of the goods effectively becomes the traders' commission. This system of transfer is very common among Somali communities across the world. In the aftermath of 9/11 attempts were made to monitor it or close it down, because of some evidence that funding for the attacks was channelled through Somalia. However, the system has proved hard to formalize, and still appears to be widespread.

Yet the 2015 sum actually represents a slowdown in remittances growth, which has increased by only 0.4 per cent since 2014. This is the slowest rate of growth of remittances since the global financial crisis from 2008–9, and is accounted for by weakening economic growth in Europe, deterioration of the Russian economy, and depreciation of the Euro and Rouble.

The top three remittance receiving countries in 2004 were India (US$70 billion), China (US$64 billion), and the Philippines (US$28 billion). However, remittances as a proportion of GDP were highest in small countries, amounting to 23 per cent in Jordan, 27 per cent in Lesotho, and 37 per cent in Tonga. It is also worth observing that compared with other developing regions, sub-Saharan Africa received the lowest level of remittances, amounting to just US$33 billion across the entire region. There is still significant debate about the impact of remittances at home. It is clear that they benefit those who receive them directly—who are often amongst the poorest in society. Remittances can lift people out of poverty: it has been estimated that in Somaliland, for example, the average household income is doubled by remittances; whilst in Lesotho they represent up to 80 per cent of the income of rural households. Besides increasing incomes remittances also diversify them, meaning that households are less reliant on a single source of income. In this way remittances also provide an insurance against risk. Often, in addition, they are spent on the education of children and health care for the elderly.

The extent to which remittances benefit those outside the immediate family, however, largely depends on how the money is spent. If used to establish small businesses, for example, or invested in community-based enterprises such as wells or schools or health clinics, then remittances can provide employment and services for people other than the direct recipients. On the other hand, if as is often the case they are spent on consumer goods such as cars and televisions, or repaying debt, their wider benefit is limited. Additionally, where some households receive remittances and others do not, disparities between households can be exacerbated and communities undermined. It is also worth remembering that migrants tend to originate in certain parts of origin countries, which means their remittances can increase regional disparities too. There is also some evidence that remittances can be used to pay migrant smugglers to help family members migrate in an irregular fashion to richer countries.

Remittances have attracted an enormous amount of positive press recently, not just in the media, but also in academic and policy circles; for example, their value for development has been recognized in the UN's 2015 Sustainable Development Goals (SDGs). But it is worth sounding a few warning bells too. First, not enough attention has been paid to the difficulties encountered through the separation of migrants from their families at home, sometimes for long periods of time. Sending money home cannot always compensate for being away from a partner, or missing out on watching children grow up, or taking care of elderly parents.

Second, the social pressures on migrants to send money home should not be underestimated. Migrants may be unemployed, in insecure jobs, or earning very low wages, and yet people back at home often expect them to send significant sums of money. Interestingly, research has demonstrated that this is often because migrants mislead their families about what they are actually doing and how much they are earning. If your parents had sold their property to be able to afford to send you to Paris, say, you might be forgiven for wanting them to believe that you had found a nice apartment and an interesting job, rather than to know you were sharing a room with six other people and cleaning the streets. Or working as a prostitute.

Finally, receiving remittances can create a 'culture of migration' in origin countries, whereby young people see the apparent rewards of migrating and place unrealistic expectations on moving abroad.

Alternatively, relying on remittances can be a disincentive for some people at home to work at all.

A particularly interesting idea to emerge from the academic literature in recent years is 'social remittances', particularly associated with the research of Peggy Levitt. What this refers to is that people send home not just money, but can also transmit new ideas, social and cultural practices, and codes of conduct. This can take place at the family level, for example, where a parent returns on holiday from working abroad and teaches a child new ideas. It can happen on a more formal basis where migrants contribute to the media in their country of origin. But perhaps the most powerful way it takes place today is via the internet. Although, as indicated in Chapter 3, access is still limited in many poor countries, opinion formers such as politicians and journalists in such countries often do use the internet, and thus can be influenced by email campaigns or discussions in internet chat rooms.

Diasporas

Where there are considerable numbers of migrants from one town or city, region, or country living together in the same country of destination, they often come together in formal organizations. These organizations take a variety of forms. They include professional associations—bringing together migrant doctors, lawyers, or teachers from the same origin, for example. They also include organizations based on common interests such as sport, religion, gender, charitable work, and development. Another type of organization is Home Town Associations (HTAs) that bring together people from the same town or city who focus their activities in development on their home town (see Box 6). As indicated in Chapter 2, the catch-all term diaspora is often used to describe these various migrant organizations.

These diaspora organizations commonly collect donations from their membership and send them back to the country of origin for

Box 6 Home Town Associations

Mexican HTAs have a long history—the most prominent were established in the 1950s. There are currently over 600 Mexican HTAs in 30 cities in the USA. They support public works in their localities of origin, including the construction of public infrastructure (for example, new roads and road repairs), donating equipment (for example, ambulances and medical equipment), and promoting education (for example, establishing scholarship programmes, constructing schools, and providing school supplies).

specific purposes; often ongoing development. They can also be for emergency assistance. Diaspora organizations rallied quickly to send home money, medical equipment, tents, and food in response to the recent Ebola outbreak in West Africa, for example.

As well as making economic contributions by sending home money and material goods, diaspora organizations can also participate in the political, social, and cultural affairs of their home country and community. The most obvious political contribution is through voting in national (and sometimes local) elections at home, from abroad. In the extraordinarily close US election in 2000, when George W. Bush narrowly defeated Al Gore, the outcome in certain states turned on the votes of overseas US citizens. During the 1993 Referendum on Independence in Eritrea, it is estimated that 98 per cent of overseas Eritreans who were entitled to vote did so. The Eritrean example provides other examples of how diaspora organizations can contribute politically. After independence, for example, representatives of Eritrean diaspora organizations were formally included in the committee responsible for drafting the country's constitution.

The contribution of diaspora organizations to social and cultural life is harder to measure, but can have an equally important impact. A good example is in Somaliland, where Somali diaspora organizations largely paid for the construction of the University of Hargeisa and Amoud University in Boorama. What is more, overseas Somali academics have returned on sabbatical arrangements to teach at the universities, and train young Somali university teachers. Technological innovation increasingly means that diaspora organizations can also contribute without physically returning, for example, through internet training programmes and video-conferencing. This is sometimes referred to as 'virtual return'.

An increasing number of countries worldwide are beginning to realize the potential contribution that diaspora organizations can make, and are making efforts to mobilize the diaspora to contribute still further. This can take place on a very formal basis—Mexico has a cabinet minister responsible for relations with overseas Mexicans. It can also take place less formally, for example, through sending representatives to lecture to organizations in various destination countries.

Just as it is worth posting certain reservations regarding remittances, so it is regarding the potential contribution of diaspora organizations. One reason is that, while diasporas can contribute to development, they can also contribute to warfare. Remittances from Ethiopian and Eritrean diaspora organizations certainly helped fund the conflict between these two countries. In addition, diaspora organizations are often dominated by a particular religious or ethnic group, and their contributions often target those particular groups, thus exacerbating disparities. An associated point is that diaspora organizations are often comprised of the educated and elite and their contributions reflect this. Building a university, for example, probably does not directly benefit poor rural peasants.

Return

Besides sending home remittances and making a collective contribution through diaspora organizations, a third way migrants can potentially contribute to development is by returning. Migrants can bring home savings from abroad to invest at home when they return, often establishing small businesses, for example. They can come home with a good network of contacts abroad that can form the basis for small-scale trade and import–export activities. As mentioned, they can also bring back new ideas which can spur entrepreneurial attitudes and activities among the people with whom they settle on return.

Once again, it is important not to overestimate the impact of return. Some people return because they have not succeeded abroad—they may come home with no savings and no new experiences and return to whatever they did before leaving. It is often the case that migrants go home to retire, having spent their working lives abroad. While they may take home money and experiences, they are not economically active themselves upon return. Also, the extent to which return has an impact really depends on conditions at home. If there is no access to land, or taxes are too high, or there is an inadequate supply of skilled labour, for example, return migrants with good intentions to set up a new business can easily become frustrated and have their plans thwarted.

As indicated in Chapters 1 and 2, there appears to be a growing tendency towards 'circular migration', whereby migrants return home for a short period of time then migrate again. There is some debate, particularly in policy circles, about whether these short-term returns can also contribute to development. Limited research among Indian workers in the Gulf States who go home for holidays suggests that their visits can provide an immediate boost to local economies. One reason is that migrants who go home for a short period of time often effectively show off—they lavish money on friends and family and engage in conspicuous consumption—buying gifts and meals and drinks.

The brain drain

Where there are high levels of unemployment at home, emigration can be positive in that it reduces competition for limited jobs. This is one reason why the government of the Philippines, for example, positively encourages emigration; another of course is the money these migrants send home.

Migration, however, can be selective, and those who leave are at times among the most entrepreneurial, best educated, and brightest in society. If their particular skills are readily available, once again this need not be a problem. India, for example, can afford computer experts and technical workers to leave in substantial numbers, as so many young people in India today have these skills. It is more usually the case, however, that these movements deplete the country of origin of skills that are scarce. This process is usually referred to as the brain drain. Besides removing skills, the brain drain also means that countries do not see any return on the investment in educating and training their own citizens.

The brain drain is a global phenomenon. For many years, for example, there have been concerns that the best scientists in Europe are leaving for North America, where salaries are higher, research grants are more generous, and equipment is better.

The process, however, has received most attention in poorer countries. Of special concern is the migration of health workers— nurses and doctors—from countries in sub-Saharan Africa. Some of the figures are startling. Only fifty out of 600 doctors trained since independence are still practising in Zambia. It has been estimated that there are currently more Malawian doctors practising in the city of Manchester in England, than in the whole of Malawi. Countries like Malawi still have high infant mortality and disease rates, and it is easy to comprehend why the absence of health workers can have such a negative impact on their development.

Although it has attracted less attention, it is also worth mentioning that there are growing concerns about the brain drain of teachers from Africa. Again, commentary on enrolment rates and literacy provided in Chapter 3 demonstrates why this should be so worrying.

Reactions to the brain drain are divided. It can be argued that the brain drain represents people moving in order to improve their lives and realize their potential, and that there is nothing wrong with that. In addition, if their own countries cannot provide adequate employment, career opportunities, and incentives to stay, then the problem lies with those countries. On the other hand, there has been criticism of the richer countries to which skilled migrants head, especially where they are actively recruiting those skills. Some countries have been accused of 'cherry-picking' the best people and leaving the rest behind. Some commentators believe that the richer countries should compensate poorer countries for their loss of skilled people. An alternative is more ethical recruitment procedures that avoid selecting staff from sectors and countries where their skills are in particularly short supply. In the longer term, as I explain in Chapter 8, temporary migration programmes, which provide for the return of migrants to their country of origin after a fixed period working abroad, may be a more sustainable response to the challenge.

Chapter 5
Irregular migration

Migrants who move in an irregular fashion leave their countries for exactly the same motivations as any other migrants. The reason that increasing numbers of migrants are moving in an irregular rather than a legal way is mainly because of increasing restrictions on legal movements, mostly in destination countries. More people than ever before want to move, but there are proportionately fewer legal opportunities for them to do so. A multi-billion dollar industry has developed around the desire of people to move despite legal restrictions, in the form of human trafficking and migrant smuggling.

What is irregular migration?

I have opted to use the terms 'irregular' migrant and 'irregular' migration, deliberately avoiding the more commonly used 'illegal'. The most powerful criticism of the term 'illegal' is that defining people as 'illegal' denies their humanity: a human being cannot be illegal. It can easily be forgotten that migrants are people and have rights whatever their legal status. Another criticism is the connotation of the term 'illegal' with criminality. Most irregular migrants are not criminals, although by definition most have breached administrative rules and regulations.

The two other terms that are often used in this context are 'undocumented' and 'unauthorized'. The former is avoided here because of its ambiguity. It is sometimes used to denote migrants who have not been documented (or recorded), and sometimes to describe migrants without documents (passports or work permits, for example). In addition, neither situation necessarily applies to all irregular migrants—many are known to the authorities and many do have documents—yet the term 'undocumented' is still often used to cover them all. Similarly, not all irregular migrants are necessarily unauthorized, and so this term too is often used imprecisely. Irregular migration is an awkward term, but the best of the commonly used alternatives.

Irregular migration is itself a complex and diverse concept that requires careful clarification. First, it is important to recognize that there are lots of ways that a migrant can become irregular. Irregular migration includes people who enter a country without the proper authority, for example, by entering without passing through a border control or entering with fraudulent documents. It also includes people who may have entered a country legally, but then remain there without permission, for example, by staying after the expiry of a visa or work permit, through sham marriages or fake adoptions, as bogus students or fraudulently self-employed. The term also includes people moved by migrant smugglers or human traffickers, and those who deliberately abuse the asylum system.

Second, there are important regional differences in the way that the concept irregular migration is applied. In Europe, for example, where the entry of people from outside the EU is closely controlled, it is relatively easy to define and identify migrants with irregular status. That is not the case in many parts of sub-Saharan Africa, where borders are porous, ethnic and linguistic groups straddle state borders, some people belong to nomadic communities, and many people do not have proof of their place of birth or citizenship.

A final complexity arises because, as indicated in Chapter 2, migrants' status can change, often quite literally overnight. A migrant can enter a country in an irregular fashion, but then regularize their status, for example, by applying for asylum or entering a regularization programme. Conversely, a migrant can enter regularly then become irregular when they work without a work permit or overstay a visa. A large number of irregular migrants in Australia, for example, are UK citizens—often students in their gap year—who have stayed beyond the expiry of their visa. Asylum-seekers can become irregular migrants when their application is rejected and they stay on without authority. More generally, a growing proportion of international migrants undertake long-distance journeys that take them from one part of the globe to another, transiting through a number of countries on their way to their final destination. In the course of a single journey, it is quite possible for a migrant to slip in and out of irregularity, according to the visa requirements of the countries concerned.

How many irregular migrants are there?

The analysis of irregular migration is further hampered by a serious lack of accurate data, making it difficult to identify trends or to compare the scale of the phenomenon in different parts of the world. One reason is conceptual—as we have seen, the term covers a range of people who can be in an irregular situation for different reasons, and people can switch from a regular to irregular status, or vice versa.

Another reason is methodological. Counting irregular migrants is virtually impossible. People without regular status are likely to avoid speaking to the authorities for fear of detection, and thus go unrecorded. Most observers agree that the majority of irregular migrants are not recorded. Various methods have been used to try to estimate numbers of irregular migrants. In some countries amnesties are periodically declared, whereby foreign nationals residing or working without legal authority can regularize their status. Direct surveys of irregular migrants have been attempted, although access is difficult. It is possible to compare different sources of recorded migration data and population data to highlight discrepancies that might be accounted for by irregular migration. Finally, surveys of employers can indirectly reveal foreign workers without legal status.

Nor is it possible, with the exception of those who are deported, to count how many irregular migrants return home. Research has indicated that it is a mistake to assume that all irregular migrants stay permanently. Many appear to come to destination countries with a specific—usually financial—target in mind, for example, to earn enough money to build a house or educate children or pay off a debt.

Another problem is access to data—however limited they may be—that have been collected. In many states such data are collected by enforcement agencies and are not made publicly available. Alternatively, information and data that may establish a person's irregular status are frequently dispersed between different agencies such as government departments, the police, and employment offices. International cooperation on data collection is even more problematic. There is no authoritative source on global trends and numbers in irregular migration, and the available sources are not comprehensive.

There is, however, a broad consensus that, as the number of international migrants has increased so too has the proportion of irregular migrants. Most estimates of irregular migration are at the national level. It is estimated, for example, that there are over 11 million irregular migrants in the USA, accounting for nearly one-third of the foreign-born population there. Over half these irregular migrants are Mexican; indeed according to some estimates about half the Mexican-born population in the USA, or almost 5 million people, are irregular migrants. It is also estimated that there are between 3.5 and 5 million irregular migrants in the Russian Federation, originating mainly in countries of the Commonwealth of Independent States (CIS) and South-East Asia. And a startling 20 million irregular migrants are thought to live in India today.

Other estimates are provided on a regional or global scale. According to estimates by the Organization for Economic Cooperation and Development (OECD), at least 5 million, or 10 per cent, of Europe's migrants are in an irregular situation, and a further half a million are estimated to enter each year. Well over 50 per cent of migrants in both Africa and Latin America are also thought to be irregular. Overall, the International Centre on Migration Policy Development (ICMPD) has estimated that 2.5 to 4 million migrants cross all international borders without authorization each year. There are, however, considerable variations in the figures provided, with sometimes very significant discrepancies between different sources.

Their unreliability notwithstanding, there is no arguing that these figures are significant. It is easy to see how they might generate concern. But it is important to place irregular migration in its proper context. In most countries, the political significance of irregular migration far outweighs its numerical significance. Even the most extreme estimates indicate that irregular migration accounts for no more than 50 per cent of all migration worldwide, and in the EU and most individual EU countries it probably accounts for no more than 10 per cent. The example of the UK is illustrative. Estimates for the number of irregular migrants entering the UK vary widely, but even the highest estimates are relatively small in comparison with regular migration to the UK. For example, 120,000 foreign students arrive each year and another 200,000 people enter legitimately to work.

It is also important to distinguish 'stocks' from 'flows'. There are few estimates of stocks of irregular migrants—no EU member state, for example, publishes official estimates of the size of its irregular population. There is no doubt, nevertheless, that in most countries stocks far outnumber new arrivals. Most irregular migrants worldwide are already present in destination countries. And very often these people have found work, have somewhere to live, and even have children at school. In other words they are already part and parcel of the societies in which they live.

The challenges of irregular migration

In political and media discourses, irregular migration is often described as constituting a threat to state sovereignty (Figure 6). Put simply, the argument is that states have a sovereign right to control who crosses their borders, and that by undermining that control irregular migrants threaten sovereignty. It follows that stopping irregular migration is fundamental to reasserting full sovereignty. In certain, more extreme discourses, irregular migration has also been perceived as a threat to state security. Specifically, irregular migration and asylum, it has been suggested, may provide channels for potential terrorists to enter countries. Given the sensitivity of the current debate, extremely careful analysis of such potentially incendiary conclusions is required.

It is important, first of all, to consider the numbers involved. Inherent in the argument that irregular migration threatens state sovereignty is the perception that states are, or risk, being overwhelmed by enormous numbers of irregular migrants. In reality in most countries it represents a fairly small proportion of total migration.

Second, irregular migrants are often ascribed tainted intentions without any substantiation. Two particularly frequent assumptions are that irregular migrants participate in illegal activities and that they are associated with the spread of infectious diseases, and especially HIV/AIDS. Both these assumptions are gross generalizations. Some irregular migrants (and asylum-seekers) are

6. Migrants at the US border fence in Tijuana, Mexico.

criminals and some carry infectious diseases—resulting, for example, from long periods spent in transit—but most do not. Misrepresenting the evidence criminalizes and demonizes all irregular migrants. It can encourage them to remain underground. It also diverts attention from those irregular migrants who actually are criminals and should be prosecuted, and those who are diseased and should be treated.

Focusing on terrorism has also meant that other equally pressing challenges associated with irregular migration—for states, societies, and importantly for migrants themselves—have often been overlooked. It is true that irregular migration can threaten state security, but this is usually in ways other than by its association with terrorism or violence. Where it involves corruption and organized crime, irregular migration can become a threat to public security. This is particularly the case where illegal entry is facilitated by migrant smugglers and human traffickers, or where criminal gangs compete for control of the labour of migrants after they have arrived.

Irregular migration can also generate xenophobic sentiments within host populations. Importantly, these sentiments are often directed not only at migrants with irregular status, but also at established migrants, refugees, and ethnic minorities. When this receives a great deal of media attention, irregular migration can also undermine public confidence in the integrity and effectiveness of a state's migration and asylum policies. Irregular migration thus can impact on the ability of governments to expand regular migration channels. The importance for a government to be perceived by its citizens to be in control cannot be underestimated. If irregular migration exists, it is not unreasonable for voters to ask why even more migration is required.

It is clear, then, that irregular migration can threaten state security, although the relationship is complex. Equally, however, irregular migration can undermine the human security of the migrants themselves. The negative consequences of irregular migration for migrants are often underestimated. It can endanger their lives. A large number of people died in 2015 trying to reach the EU. And one of the great unknowns of international migration is how many people there are who have left their homes but not yet reached their intended destinations, and what their lives are like in transit countries.

Women constitute a substantial proportion of the many migrants with irregular status. Because they are confronted with gender-based discrimination, female migrants with irregular status are often obliged to accept the most menial informal sector jobs. Such can be the level of abuse of their human rights that some commentators have compared contemporary human trafficking with the slave trade. Women in particular also face specific health-related risks, including exposure to HIV/AIDS. More generally, people who enter or remain in a country without authorization are often at risk of exploitation by employers and landlords. And because of their irregularity, migrants are usually unable to make full use of their skills and experience once they have arrived in a country of destination.

Migrants with irregular status are often unwilling to seek redress from authorities because they fear arrest and deportation. As a result, they do not always make use of public services to which they are entitled, for example, emergency healthcare. In most countries, they are also barred from using the full range of services available to citizens and migrants with regular status. In such situations, already hard-pressed NGOs, religious bodies, and other civil society institutions are obliged to provide assistance to migrants with irregular status, at times compromising their own legality.

7. Migrants climbing over a fence in Frethun in Northern France to board a freight train bound for the Channel Tunnel and the UK.

Irregular migration is a particularly emotive issue, and one that tends to polarize opinion. Those who are concerned about border control and national security are often opposed by those whose main concern is the human rights of the migrants concerned (Figure 7). Another challenge is therefore to encourage an objective debate on the causes and consequences of irregular migration and the ways in which it might be most effectively addressed.

Human trafficking and migrant smuggling

Human trafficking and migrant smuggling probably comprise a relatively small proportion of irregular migration worldwide, but they have attracted such attention recently that it is worth devoting the remainder of this chapter to these issues. Briefly four questions are answered. What are human trafficking and migrant smuggling? What is the scale? What are the costs involved? And what are the consequences for the migrants themselves?

Although the two concepts are often confused, even by policy-makers and academics, there is a legal distinction between human trafficking and migrant smuggling. The trafficking of human beings is defined by the UN Protocol to Prohibit, Suppress and Punish Trafficking in Persons (1999) as:

> The recruitment, transportation, transfer, harbouring or receipt of persons, by means of the threat, or use of force or other forms of coercion, of abduction, of fraud, of deception, of the abuse of power or of a position of vulnerability or of the giving or receiving of payments or benefits to achieve the consent of a person having control over another person, for the purpose of exploitation.

The trafficking of women—and sometimes even children—to work as prostitutes or in the sex trade has attracted most attention. It is hard to research trafficking, but according to studies by IOM what appears typically to happen is that young women are promised the opportunity to work abroad. A price is agreed which the woman will pay in instalments after she starts working. She is then transported, usually illegally, to a destination country, where she finds that she is forced to work as a prostitute, and that virtually all her income is taken by the trafficker. There are also reports of young women and children being kidnapped from their homes and transported away against their will. Indeed some people depict human trafficking as a modern version of slavery.

The smuggling of migrants is defined as: 'The procurement, in order to obtain, directly or indirectly a financial or other material benefit, of the illegal entry of a person into a state party of which the person is not a national or a permanent resident.' In contrast to human trafficking, migrant smuggling is largely voluntary. It involves potential migrants, or more often their family, paying a smuggler to move them to a destination country illegally. After they have arrived their association with the smuggler normally ends, so that they are not subsequently open to exploitation in the way that victims of trafficking are.

In reality there can be a blurring of the boundaries between human trafficking and migrant smuggling. This occurs in particular where migrants do not pay a smuggler before migrating, which means they arrive in the destination country in debt to the smuggler. This in turn opens up the possibility of exploitation.

Just as with irregular migration more generally, it is impossible to enumerate accurately either human trafficking or migrant smuggling. Figures provided are usually for people who are found and who admit to having been smuggled or trafficked. The problem is that no one knows what proportion of trafficked and smuggled people are actually found. It seems reasonable to assume that many are never known to the authorities.

According to the International Labour Organization (ILO) there are almost 21 million victims of human trafficking worldwide, including 5.5 million children. Over 50 per cent of these victims were in the Asia-Pacific region, followed in rank order by Africa then Latin America. The developed economies and EU account for 1.5 million victims of trafficking. ILO estimates that human trafficking generates US$150 billion per year.

By definition, human trafficking has negative consequences for the people involved. Human traffickers ruthlessly exploit migrants. Victims of human trafficking are not free to decide on the activities in which they engage. They are often forced into low-paid, insecure, and degrading work from which they may find it impossible to escape and for which they receive trivial or no compensation. While a great deal of recent attention has been given to the trafficking of women, it is important to note that this phenomenon also affects men and children. Migrant children with irregular migration status who are separated from their parents are a particularly vulnerable group, and may be trafficked into the sex industry.

Turning now to migrant smuggling, research I was involved in for the Migration Research Unit at University College London tried to estimate global costs for migrant smuggling. It reviewed over 600 sources in which the costs charged to migrants were reported. Naturally this was an exercise riddled with problems, and the results are no more than estimates, but they do provide interesting reading (Table 2).

For the purposes of the discussion here there are three points worth emphasizing. One is just how much smugglers and traffickers can charge. The average cost reported for a journey from Asia to the Americas is over US$26,000. One implication is that increasingly it is only the relatively well off who can afford to pay smugglers and to move. US$26,000 is a very significant sum of money in a country like Pakistan, for example, where many of the incidents of migration between Asia and the Americas were reported to originate.

Table 2 The costs of migrant smuggling

Routes	Mean costs (US$)
Asia–Americas	26,041
Europe–Asia	16,462
Asia–Australasia	14,011
Asia–Asia	12,240
Asia–Europe	9,374
Europe–Australasia	7,400
Africa–Europe	6,533
Europe–Americas	6,389
Americas–Europe	4,528
Americas–Americas	2,984
Europe–Europe	2,708
Africa–Americas	2,200
Africa–Australasia	1,951
Africa–Africa	203

A second observation is the wide range of costs involved. At the bottom end of the scale, the cost for being smuggled across a border in Africa was as low as US$203, although even this can be a significant sum given the income levels in these countries described in Chapter 3. In several cases reported, payments for smuggling between African countries were made not in cash but, for example, with bags of rice and other goods. A final message to take from the table is again that smuggling is a global phenomenon, not just a process from 'South' to 'North'.

By looking at reports on the costs of migrant smuggling over a period of years, the research also tried to see whether costs have been increasing or decreasing. Although there are variations between the main routes, the overall impression is that costs are decreasing gradually. This would seem to be because there is increasing competition in the smuggling business, with smugglers constantly undercutting one another and adjusting their methods to attract more customers (see Box 7).

A final aspect of the research on costs was to try to understand what the main determinants of costs are. One was distance travelled—longer journeys cost more. A second was the mode of transport: flying is more expensive than travelling by sea, which is in turn costlier than going overland. A third main determinant

Box 7 Migrant smuggling as a business

I have spent periods over the last decade interviewing migrant smugglers in Afghanistan and Pakistan. They reported that over time not only had the amount they charge changed, but also the way they received payments had too. About ten years ago, migrant smugglers apparently insisted that payments were made in full in advance. The danger for migrants was that smugglers might take their money and disappear before moving them. In response to these fears, some smugglers changed their practice, asking only for a deposit in advance of movement, with the balance to be repaid after arrival in the destination country. The problem here was that some migrants were exploited by smugglers to whom they were indebted after they had arrived. Now smugglers have responded to their clients' concerns and demands once again. Now, payment is made in full in advance, but is deposited with a third party rather than being paid to the smuggler directly. The money is released to the smuggler only after the migrant has called to confirm he or she has arrived safely in their destination. What this amounts to is a money-back guarantee on migrant smuggling.

appeared to be the number of people travelling—the more people who travel at the same time, the less each appears to be charged.

Smuggling also poses risks for those involved. Smugglers can charge many thousands of dollars to transport them from one place to another. Smugglers do not always inform migrants in advance of where they will be taken. The means of transport used by migrant smugglers are often unsafe, and migrants who are travelling in this way may find themselves abandoned by their smuggler and unable to complete the journey they have paid for (see Box 8). Using the services of smugglers, many migrants have drowned at sea, suffocated in sealed containers, or have been raped and abused while in transit.

Box 8   The experiences of Suleiman, interviewed in Kabul in 2003

'The first time I was smuggled abroad, the plan was to fly to Dushanbe then continue overland to Moscow. The first stage was fine—I boarded the airplane in Karachi with a fake Pakistani passport without any problems. The agent who accompanied me to the airport told me that at the airport in Dushanbe I would be met by another agent, named Nafi. When I arrived in Dushanbe, however, I was arrested as soon as I stepped off the aeroplane. I was imprisoned for four weeks—with other Afghan illegal migrants, interrogated, beaten regularly, and threatened with torture. After a month, for no apparent reason, I was collected one night from my cell and driven back to the airport at Dushanbe. Nafi was waiting for me. Nafi explained that on the flight from Karachi with me had been another 50 illegal immigrants, their journeys organized by several other agents in Pakistan. One agent had failed to bribe immigration officials at Dushanbe airport, so they had arrested those they understood to be the "clients" of that particular agent. I had been arrested as a result of mistaken identity.'

Chapter 6
Refugees and asylum-seekers

An asylum-seeker is a person who has applied for international protection. Most do so once they have reached the country in which they are seeking protection, although it is possible to apply for asylum outside the country where you are seeking protection, for example, at an embassy or a consulate. Asylum-seekers' applications are judged by the criteria of the 1951 United Nations Convention relating to the Status of Refugees, which is discussed in detail in the following section. Successful applicants are granted refugee status and become refugees. Unsuccessful applicants can normally appeal, and if their appeal is unsuccessful they are expected to leave the country. In Europe and North America there are also a range of other statuses, usually grouped together under the description of Exceptional Leave to Remain (ELR), that are granted to people who are not refugees but still cannot return to their homes.

The international refugee regime

The international refugee regime comprises a series of laws that define refugees and determine their rights and obligations, and a series of norms to which, although not necessarily legally binding, states are expected to adhere. This regime is implemented and monitored by a number of institutions.

8. **Rwandan refugees on the move.**

The critical legal convention is the 1951 United Nations
Convention relating to the Status of Refugees. It defines a
refugee as someone who 'owing to a well-founded fear of being
persecuted for reasons of race, religion, nationality, membership
of a particular social group or political opinion, is outside the
country of his nationality' (Figure 8). Although certain variations
on this basic definition have been agreed in both Africa and
Latin America, it is still essentially the definition that is applied
worldwide.

A number of aspects of this definition have attracted considerable
debate. First, it is worth noting how dated the Convention is—it
was written over sixty years ago. Many critics argue that, while the
refugee definition may well have been adequate then, it no longer
addresses the realities of refugees in the modern world. For
example, the Convention focuses on persecution by the state, and
this is because it was written mainly to protect those who had
been persecuted by the Nazi regime. During the cold war the
definition also served a political purpose, when it was applied in
particular to those fleeing Communism. But often in the world

today refugees flee the general insecurity of conflict rather than specific political persecution.

In addition, the Convention does not explicitly cover people who have been persecuted on the basis of their sex or sexuality. We need look no further than the experiences of women and homosexuals under the Taliban regime in Afghanistan to understand how important this can be today. Nor does it cover people who flee for broadly environmental reasons, for example, in response to a tsunami or earthquake. Yet there is a plausible argument that fleeing such hazards is often a symptom of a political failure—for example, to predict the hazard, or mitigate or insure against its effects, or provide adequate shelter and protection in its aftermath—and that in this sense these people might also fall within the refugee definition.

A third observation is that the definition applies only to people outside their country of nationality. There are far more people, however, who have fled their homes but been unable to leave their countries; they are normally referred to as Internally Displaced Persons (IDPs). There is a good case to be made that IDPs are even more vulnerable than refugees—they have not even been able to find a way out of their own country and thus escape persecution, and they are not protected by an international regime in the same way that refugees are. Despite these reservations, other commentators feel that the 1951 Convention should be upheld. First, it does still cover the majority of those people outside their country who need protection—relatively few people fall through the gaps. Second, the Office of the United Nations High Commissioner for Refugees (UNHCR), which is responsible for implementing the Convention, does in practice extend the definition of a refugee to cover those who are excluded but still clearly in need of protection, including where possible IDPs and those fleeing natural disasters. Third, some 160 states worldwide have signed the Convention, and most people agree that it is very unlikely that so many countries would sign a revised version or new convention.

A series of norms also govern state responses to refugees. These derive either in law from the 1951 Convention or other legal instruments (such as the 1948 Universal Declaration of Human Rights), or in non-binding but widely applied customary law or agreements. Foremost among these norms are: the right to leave one's own country, the right to access the territory of other states, that asylum be provided as a non-political act, that refugees should not be returned to their own country forcibly (*non refoulement*), that full economic and social rights should be extended to refugees, and that states are obliged to try to provide lasting solutions for refugees. Equally refugees have obligations, primarily to obey the law of the country providing asylum.

The 1951 Convention is upheld, implemented, and monitored by the UNHCR. Gil Loescher's book *The UNHCR and World Politics* provides a fascinating overview of how UNHCR and the international refugee regime have evolved. He describes how in 1951, when he was appointed the first United Nations High Commissioner for Refugees, Gerrit Jan van Heuven Goedhart 'found three empty rooms and a secretary', was given a narrow mandate that was expected to last for only three years, and had control over virtually no funds. In 2015, in contrast, Antonio Guterres, the tenth High Commissioner, is in control of an agency with an annual budget of over US$7 billion, a staff of around 6,000 and a mandate that arguably makes UNHCR the leading humanitarian organization in the world.

Today UNHCR suffers a perennial funding crisis. The agency, unlike some other UN bodies, receives only a minimal allocation from central UN funds and instead is expected to raise its annual budget. It has tended to rely on a few major donors, most significantly the USA, the European Commission, Sweden, Japan, the Netherlands, and the UK. The funding crisis for UNHCR is compounded by the fact that it has extended its activities beyond refugees specifically to also cover other populations of concern.

The International Organization for Migration (IOM), which is outside the UN system, is also an important institution in the international refugee regime. It is largely responsible for logistics, especially transporting refugees. The efforts of UNHCR and IOM are supported by a wide range of non-governmental organizations (NGOs) which often take direct responsibility for aspects of camp management, food distribution, healthcare, and education.

The global geography of refugees

The global geography of refugees has changed considerably since the international refugee regime came into force. The initial challenge was to try to find solutions for those who had fled Nazi persecution in Germany and occupied Europe. Many of these people were eventually resettled in the USA. UNHCR and the 1951 Convention were originally intended to function for a limited time period, and to cease once these initial activities had been successfully concluded. Events, however, took over. By the 1960s major new refugee populations were being generated in Africa, largely as a result of decolonization. Many of these refugees settled permanently in neighbouring African countries. In the 1970s the geographical focus of the refugee regime shifted again, to South and South-East Asia, as a result of the birth of the state of Bangladesh in 1971 and war in Vietnam and elsewhere in Indochina. Some of these refugees were eventually resettled in Europe. In the 1980s Central America briefly became the main geographical focus.

What is striking about the 1990s is that refugees were being generated simultaneously in both the developed and developing world. Major refugee flows in the 1990s originated simultaneously in Bosnia, Kosovo, the former Soviet Union, the Horn of Africa,

Rwanda, Iraq, Afghanistan, and East Timor. At the same time major refugee returns were taking place in Mozambique and Namibia and towards the end of the 1990s in Afghanistan and Bosnia too. Furthermore, for the first time, significant numbers of refugees began to travel outside their own regions to seek asylum in the developed world. What had begun as a largely European problem at the end of the Second World War had become a truly global phenomenon, with immense complexities.

The first edition of this book reported that the number of refugees worldwide was the lowest for twenty-five years; present figures are the highest for at least fifty years. In 2014 UNHCR reported almost 20 million refugees, and this number had certainly increased in 2015 in particular as a result of the crisis in Syria. The most important countries of origin for refugees in 2014 were Syria, Afghanistan, and Somalia. The most important host countries were Turkey, Pakistan, and Lebanon. Overall, developing regions hosted 86 per cent of the world's refugees in 2014. The dramatic increase is a result of ongoing crises in Syria, Afghanistan, and North Africa, combined with a sharp reduction in the number of people who have been able to go home. In 2014 only 120,000 refugees returned home—the lowest return rate since 1983. In addition to these 20 million refugees worldwide, UNHCR reported almost 40 million IDPs and 1.8 million asylum-seekers in 2014; as well as almost 10 million stateless people. The cautious optimism about the future of refugees expressed in the first edition of this book needs to be revisited.

Causes of refugee movements

The 1951 Convention definition of a refugee emphasizes the concept of persecution in explaining why refugees flee their homes. There are certainly still some predatory regimes in the world today that actively persecute segments of their national population—North Korea is an example that would be hard to refute. However, it seems that most refugees today flee conflict rather than direct persecution by the state. In the words of Aristide Zolberg, one of the leading theorists of refugee movements, they 'escape violence', not necessarily persecution. The reason they are still defined as refugees is that, even if the state is not persecuting them directly, it is still not capable of protecting them and providing them with the rights to which citizens are universally entitled.

Although this is not the place to review the extensive literature on modern warfare, it is worth listing the characteristics that the influential scholar Mary Kaldor has described as distinguishing 'new wars' from previous conflicts, as they have implications for refugee movements. First, and in contrast to most people's immediate conceptions about war, almost all conflicts today are fought within states along ethnic or religious lines, and not between states. The conflict between Eritrea and Ethiopia from 1998 to 2000 was an unusual exception. Second, warfare has become 'informalized' or 'privatized', meaning that increasingly it is fought not by professional armies, but by militias or mercenary groups. Third, whereas warfare used mainly to kill combatants, today it kills chiefly civilians. It is estimated that in modern warfare up to 90 per cent of casualties are civilians, compared with a rate of about 25 per cent in the First World War. Fourth, and especially in Africa, modern conflicts tend to endure or recur. One reason is that they are often based on ethnic divisions, which last beyond any peace settlement and can be reignited. Another is that demobilization often fails—an abundance of weapons combined with hundreds of thousands of unemployed, bored, and aggressive young men can be an incendiary mix.

A final characteristic of new wars is rising refugee ratios, and three reasons are identified. One is that the displacement of populations has become a strategic goal in warfare, and at times warring parties will even cooperate to achieve the relocation of particular populations. The so-called 'ethnic cleansing' that occurred in the Balkans during the 1990s is a case in point. Another is that modern weaponry allows more people to be terrorized (or killed) more quickly. Finally, the widespread use of land mines often leaves people no option but to leave their land during conflict.

Consequences of refugee movements

There is a fairly vast academic literature and body of agency reports dealing with the consequences of refugee movements, ranging from psychological implications for refugees through the environmental impacts of refugee camps to the prevalence of HIV/ AIDS among refugees. The best single source for up-to-date data, research, and policy on the entire range of issues is the website of UNHCR (*www.unhcr.org*). Rather than even attempt to capture the essence of so many dimensions, this section focuses instead on three cross-cutting themes: patterns and processes of settlement, gender, and aid.

Refugee camps have attracted significant attention, and tend to divide opinions. Most organizations, and some experts, view them as essential for protecting refugees and the best way to deliver assistance and education. Others point out that violence and sexual abuse can occur frequently in camps, they can generate dependency among refugees, and they can quickly have a deleterious impact on the local environment, for example, through draining or polluting ground water and deforestation. Camps can also have a deep psychological impact on refugees when they live in them for protracted periods—in some cases many years (see Box 9).

Not all refugees settle in camps—probably at least in part because of some of the problems associated with them. A significant proportion of refugees 'self-settles' within the local population, normally in villages close to the border. This is particularly the case where refugees find themselves within the same ethnic group despite having crossed an international border, which is often the case in Africa. Even harder to identify and study

Box 9 Protracted refugee situations

Protracted refugee situations are of growing concern to UNHCR. The agency defines these as situations in which 'refugees find themselves in a long-lasting and intractable state of limbo. Their lives may not be at risk, but their basic rights and essential economic, social and psychological needs remain unfulfilled after years in exile. A refugee in this situation is often unable to break free from enforced reliance on external assistance.' In 2014 UNHCR estimated that there were thirty-nine different protracted situations in the world, accounting for some 11 million refugees in total. Specific initiatives have been established for Bhutanese refugees in Nepal, Afghan refugees in Pakistan and Iran, and Somali refugees in Kenya, Yemen, Ethiopia, and Djibouti.

are refugees who live in cities—Khartoum in Sudan and Cairo in Egypt are each estimated to be home to hundreds of thousands of refugees.

It appears that refugees adopt settlement strategies that can combine all three options of camps, self-settlement, and urban dwellings. In some cases refugee families divide themselves, so that young men go to the city to work while women and children stay in the camp and receive assistance. Alternatively, entire families move between places to try to maximize their income and security.

There tend to be more women than men among refugee populations. One reason is that men are more likely to be killed in conflict or conscripted, or to risk staying at home to try to defend land and property or keep working. Yet it was not until relatively recently that refugee women attracted serious and increasing academic attention, and the present tendency is for the literature to focus fairly exclusively on the challenges faced by them. Refugee women can be subject to violence and sexual abuse at the hands of frustrated husbands and other men with the consequent health risks; the responsibility of care-giving falls disproportionately on them, especially in female-headed households; they are also responsible for cooking—most graphically illustrated by the increasing distances that women have to walk to collect firewood, and so on.

Susan Forbes Martin's *Refugee Women* focused attention specifically on refugee women, but also emphasized that they are often the most resourceful and enterprising within refugee settlements. Her book has been credited with changing the way that UNHCR in particular approaches the issue of refugee women. Where possible, it is often now considered preferable to distribute food and other items directly to women; they are also often trained as peer educators within refugee communities. Indeed, migration is often portrayed as an empowering process for women (including refugees), and one concern is that they can lose their power once they return home to traditional patriarchal societies.

An important debate that surrounds refugee aid is whether, when, and how to provide assistance to refugees. Without doubt the key book in this debate is Barbara Harrell-Bond's *Imposing Aid*, a seminal text in the academic field of refugee studies. Although many people consider her case to be overstated, she launches a convincing and scathing critique of the aid regime in refugee camps. For example, that there may be times when aid is no longer necessary, and generates dependence; that there have been instances where inappropriate aid has been provided—for example, foodstuffs that offend the majority of the population being assisted; that refugee men are not necessarily the best recipients of aid, as they have been known to cash in aid to fund other activities, thus depriving their family of food.

Durable solutions

There are three so-called durable solutions for refugees. Each can be problematic and none is working well at the moment, as demonstrated by rising numbers of refugees, the increasing proportion of protracted refugee situations, and fewer returns.

The solution normally considered the best is voluntary repatriation—in other words for refugees to return home. An initial comment is to place the emphasis on the term 'voluntary'. Although *non refoulement* is a central tenet in refugee protection, there are cases where refugees are returned against their will and before it is safe for them to go home. Another potential dilemma for repatriation is how to define home. Is it, for example, appropriate to return refugees to a place in their country of origin that is safe, even if their specific region of origin is still unsafe? UNHCR says no, but an increasing number of states say yes.

A significant unknown in refugee repatriation is what happens to refugees after they go home. By virtue of the stipulations of the 1951 Convention refugees are no longer entitled to special protection or assistance once they have crossed the border home, although as we have seen UNHCR does extend assistance to some returnees. The potential obstacles for these people should not be underestimated. They usually do not have a job to return to. Their homes and land have often been taken by someone else in their absence, or destroyed or mined. The infrastructure—roads, schools, hospitals—is often destroyed. They can face harassment from demobilized soldiers and envy and resentment from those who did not flee the country. And some, especially women and children, face the psychological challenges of coming to terms with often diminished status within the community.

A second solution is local integration, where refugees settle permanently in the host country. In the 1960s and 1970s this was a fairly common solution in Africa in particular. As already intimated, it was often the case that refugees crossed borders but stayed among their own ethnic group. This, in addition to the fact that in this era their numbers were relatively small, meant that settling locally was relatively unproblematic. Indeed, in countries like Tanzania, refugees helped boost local economies by settling in villages and towns.

Local integration is far less common in Africa today, where host governments are increasingly hostile to refugee populations. One reason is their sheer numbers. Another is that refugees are increasingly perceived as importing problems—competition for land and jobs, for example, and environmental degradation. Increasingly African and other developing countries expect refugees to return home once it is safe to do so.

In contrast, in the developed world refugee status has traditionally conferred permanent residence rights. Although legally refugees can be expected to return home when they can, in practice almost all refugees in Europe, for example, remain permanently. In the UK, a refugee can apply for British citizenship seven years after receiving refugee status.

Third-country resettlement is the final durable solution. This describes the process whereby refugees, usually from camps, are resettled permanently in another country, almost always in the developed world. The USA, Australia, and Canada resettle most refugees. Refugee resettlement was fairly common in Europe through the 1970s and 1980s; this was when many Vietnamese 'boat people' and refugees from Pinochet's Chile arrived there. Today, however, quotas for resettlement in Europe are grossly inadequate. The problem is that, in the current climate of public concern about asylum-seekers and refugees in certain quarters in Europe, large-scale resettlement is not a politically viable option, although it is being discussed once again in response to the Syrian refugee crisis.

Asylum in the industrialized world

Asylum-seekers have risen to the top of political agendas across the industrialized world, in particular in Europe, and there is a perception in certain parts of the media and sometimes among the public of an impending crisis (Figure 9). On the one hand, it is possible to argue that this crisis has been exaggerated. On the other hand, there are some important challenges associated with asylum in the industrialized world that are worthy of separate attention even in a global overview of refugees and asylum-seekers.

The issue of asylum began to attract increasing attention in Europe in particular at the beginning of the 1990s. This was when the number of asylum-seekers arriving there peaked—at around 700,000 in 1992. Their numbers, furthermore, were compounded by the arrival of almost one million refugees in Western Europe fleeing the war in Bosnia.

Besides numbers, several other characteristics of asylum-seekers at this time added to unease. First, they were arriving without authorization—the term 'spontaneous' asylum-seekers is often used. During the 1970s and 1980s Europe had resettled refugees, as we have seen, but their number, character, and manner of arrival could be controlled by the destination countries. In contrast, asylum-seekers simply arrived at borders, and often from distant countries—Afghanistan, Somalia, and Sri Lanka were all important origin countries at the time. Second, and again in contrast with resettled refugees, many of those applying for asylum were in fact not refugees at all. As legal opportunities to migrate to Europe to work had been reduced in the 1980s, asylum became one of the few channels for would-be labour migrants to arrive in Europe. A final concern that was widely expressed at the time was that these people would therefore be the harbingers of massive migration from the South to the North.

9. *Daily Express* front page from 2014.

It was largely in response to rising numbers as well as these other concerns that states across Europe introduced a raft of new policies to try to reduce the number of asylum-seekers and ensure that those who did arrive had a genuine claim and were not 'bogus': visas were imposed on nationals of many countries. Airlines and other carriers were required to check the passports and visas of all passengers and fined if they did not. Asylum procedures were streamlined to try to process applications more quickly. Access to welfare benefits for asylum-seekers was restricted.

There is considerable debate about the impact of such policies. Certainly the number of asylum-seekers in Europe decreased significantly—in 2004 there were only 233,000 asylum applications in the EU, considerably less than half the number reported for those same countries in 1992. By 2014, however, the number of asylum seekers in Europe had rebounded to over 700,000, exceeding 1992 levels. Some commentators have suggested that asylum trends are determined by circumstances in countries of origin rather than by policies in destination countries. It has also been argued that, while new policies may at least initially reduce the number of people seeking asylum, they continue to arrive but now do so in an irregular fashion—irregular migration has begun to replace asylum.

The catch-all term the 'migration–asylum nexus' is increasingly used to describe the particular challenges of asylum in the industrialized world today. It refers to the conceptual and policy challenges of distinguishing refugees from 'bogus' applicants, on the one hand, and asylum-seekers from irregular migrants, on the other.

The UK is illustrative of these challenges. In the UK over the last decade, about 10–20 per cent of asylum-seekers have been considered to satisfy the criteria in the 1951 Convention and granted refugee status. A further 20–30 per cent of asylum-seekers do not satisfy the Convention criteria, but they are granted the temporary status of ELR because it is accepted that it is currently unsafe for them to return to their country of origin. This means that somewhere between 50 and 70 per cent of asylum-seekers are not recognized as being in need of protection. Those rejected have the right to appeal, and some are subsequently granted protection. The majority have their appeals rejected, and are then obliged to return to their countries of origin. But many do not, staying in the UK illegally.

The situation of rejected asylum-seekers remaining in the destination country despite having had their applications and subsequent appeals rejected is one way that asylum has become conflated with irregular migration (see Box 10). Another is that increasing proportions of asylum-seekers today appear to arrive and enter in an irregular manner, often with the assistance of migrant smugglers. Given some of the dangers associated with migrant smuggling described in Chapter 5, this is of great concern to asylum advocates and human rights organizations. Finally, some also break the law once they have arrived, usually by working before they are given a work permit.

In this context, it is perhaps not surprising that the terms 'asylum-seeker' and 'irregular migrant' are often used

Box 10 Returning rejected asylum-seekers

The UK has a particularly bad track record of returning rejected asylum-seekers. In 2006 the UK Home Office estimated that there were between 150,000 and 288,000 rejected asylum-seekers still living in the UK, and that it would take up to eighteen years to return them. The main problem is locating these individuals—many disappear within communities of their own ethnic groups, often working illegally. At the same time the UK government has had to strike a tacit balancing act between the benefits of returning rejected asylum-seekers, and the risk that their returns might encourage resentment within the UK's significant settled ethnic minorities. There is also a vociferous anti-deportation campaign in the UK that is concerned— sometimes justifiably—that rejected asylum-seekers may nevertheless be returned to countries where they face persecution.

interchangeably. The problem is that this diverts attention from the fact that a good proportion of asylum-seekers are genuinely fleeing for their life or liberty and seeking protection. The concern is that refugees—people who are entitled to protection under the international refugee regime—are endangering their lives to access the asylum system in the industrialized world, and that once there they are increasingly perceived as and treated like irregular migrants.

Chapter 7
Migrants in society

One of the most pressing contemporary debates concerns the impacts of immigration on destination societies. Large and rising numbers of immigrants have been entering advanced industrial societies at the same time that many of these societies are faced with immense structural changes. These include economic, demographic, and technological changes that are transforming society, the labour market, and community. Among their outcomes have been painful changes in social safety nets despite growing needs, burgeoning physical infrastructure demands, and brewing social and cultural crises. The wider context is of global economic uncertainties particularly in the aftermath of the global financial crisis, and a heightened sense of insecurity.

Immigration and immigrants provide a tangible, visible, and convenient explanation for the malaises of modern society. This is one reason why there is rising support for the far right across many industrialized nations. The balance of the vast academic literature on the impacts of migration on society is, however, ambiguous. It stresses that a static approach may not fully reflect the realities of the impacts of immigration, which is likely to vary over time, for example, as immigrants acquire new skills and experience in the labour market. It emphasizes that it can be very difficult to isolate the effect of migration on change and separate it from other aspects that also attract popular protest such as trade liberalization and privatization. It also suggests that the impact of migrants and migration varies significantly according to a wide range of factors including the characteristics of migrants, their geographical location in host societies, and underlying labour market conditions and social relations there. Furthermore, it is hard to quantify the cost or benefit of the non-economic impacts of immigration, on politics, society, culture, and so on.

The economic impact of immigration

The economic impact of immigration in destination societies is a hotly contested field. Academic debates are, on the whole, more sophisticated in the USA than Europe, partly because until recently the political and economic climate in Europe has made it difficult to argue the case for the positive economic benefits of immigration. This was not always the case; the logic behind the *Gastarbeiter* system in Germany during the 1950s and 1960s, for example, was almost entirely one of economic benefits.

The primary debate has been about the impact of immigration on economic growth, and it is still ongoing and unresolved. Proponents who argue that the impact is positive point to longstanding evidence of the willingness of migrants to take low-wage jobs, the high levels of ambition that many immigrants demonstrate, and the flexibility that comes from having a regular supply of labour (see Box 11). It is also argued that immigrants increase returns on capital investments, have a minimal effect on other wages, that their entrepreneurship generates jobs, and that their labour can enable a country to remain competitive in an industry that would otherwise lose out to international competition. In some cases the positive effect of migration on countries of origin is also included on this side of the debate, the key aspects of which have already been explained in Chapter 4.

Other equally respected experts in the USA and elsewhere make just as convincing a case that immigration can have a negative

Box 11 Historical experiences

Several episodes in recent history provide interesting precedents for assessing the economic impacts of immigration. In 1962, 900,000 people of European origin living in Algeria moved to France, increasing the French labour force by 1.6 per cent. Analysis found that at most the impact was to reduce wages in the regions where they settled by 0.8 per cent and raise the unemployment rate by 0.2 percentage points. In 1974, 600,000 colonists returned to Portugal from the African colonies of Angola and Mozambique. Empirical analysis was unable to discern any impact on the labour market. In 1980 around 125,000 Cubans entered Miami, increasing the labour force by 7 per cent. When the impact of their immigration on resident unskilled labour from different ethnicities was assessed, only the Cubans appeared to have been negatively affected.

economic impact. They point to higher levels of unemployment among the foreign-born, the prevalence of large family sizes with the attendant welfare costs, and the negative effects of competition with established minorities. A pool of low-skilled labour can also defer the restructuring and reorganization of industries; it can create sweatshop labour conditions and undercut the power of trade unions to maintain labour standards.

Within the general debate on the economic impact of migration, three aspects have attracted particular attention, namely impacts on the availability of jobs for the native-born and on the level of their wages, and fiscal effects, especially on public sector costs.

One of the most abiding fears expressed in destination countries around the world is that migrants will take away jobs from the native-born. This concern is especially evident in many European countries, where unemployment levels are relatively high and the proportion of long-term unemployed among the unemployed relatively large. In reality, however, this appears to be rarely the case. That is because in most countries in the world migrants are admitted to fill gaps in the local labour market (this is not true for refugees who are admitted on the basis of humanitarian not economic criteria). These can be skills gaps which the local training and education system has been unable to fill, or low-status jobs that locals are unwilling to do. Migrant workers are rarely encouraged to enter situations to compete directly with local workers. Extensive comparative research across the industrialized nations indicates that the impact of immigration on jobs for local populations is at worst neutral and at best positive in that it can create economic growth and more jobs (see Box 12).

Box 12 Self-employed foreign workers and ethnic entrepreneurs

There is a growing literature on self-employed foreign workers, who are numerous in Canada, Denmark, Finland, Spain, Ireland, and the UK. Three main explanations for high levels of self-employment among immigrants in such countries are common. One is based on the selective nature of migration, that immigrants are more dynamic and less reluctant to take risks than the native-born. Another argument, conversely, is that migrants become self-employed because of barriers to securing salaried jobs, including discrimination, language obstacles, and poor access to information. The development of economic activities aimed at immigrants' communities of origin is a third explanation, and the concept of ethnic entrepreneurship is often used to describe these community-type activities. Importantly, their impact often extends beyond a specific ethnic community, for example, Indian, Italian, and Turkish culinary specialities were largely introduced by immigrants for immigrants but are now an integral part of eating habits all over the world.

A key aspect of the immigration debate in the USA has focused on the impact on wage levels. At a national and aggregate level, the consensus that has emerged is that negative effects are most likely to be felt for those whose labour market characteristics are most like migrants, in other words for those who are in direct competition with migrants for work. This effect, it is argued, is offset by positive effects on the wages for those who are not competing with migrants for work because they benefit from the greater profitability of US firms as a result of immigration.

With the growth in the US of low-skilled migration in recent years, attention has focused in particular on the effects of immigration on the wages of native-born low-skilled workers. African Americans are over-represented among the less skilled and are highly vulnerable within the labour market as a whole, so the possible effects of immigration on them are especially salient. The results of recent research are not entirely clear or consistent. On the one hand, studies conducted in New York have shown a declining relative position for African American males in terms of labour market participation and earnings in the 1980s and early 1990s, at exactly the same time that the highest levels of immigration were recorded, much of it involving the low-skilled. On the other hand, few studies have been able to demonstrate a net effect that can be attributed solely to immigration. In other words, immigration is normally one of a variety of factors that might account for the depression of wages, and it is hard to isolate its effect.

A final aspect of the debate on the economic impact of immigration concerns its effect on public finances. Separate studies in Australia, Germany, the UK, and the USA have found the overall effect to be positive; that on aggregate immigrants generate more in taxes paid than they cost in services received. The normal explanations are that there is a skewed age structure within most migrant communities, which are dominated by people of an economically active age, and in general there are high levels of employment among migrants. In addition, the destination country has not normally had to bear the cost of rearing, educating, and training the migrants. In many cases, furthermore, they do not have to bear the cost of old age dependency either, as migrants often return home when they retire.

There are important variations. Studies suggest, for example, that the fiscal impact of immigration is less clearly positive in countries like the USA which do not face an acute ageing population problem, as compared with many European countries and Japan which do. A study in New Zealand found that, while overall immigration makes a positive fiscal contribution to government revenues, new migrants from Asia and the Pacific Islands specifically cost more than they contribute in taxes.

A key factor in all these aspects of the debate on the economic impacts of immigration is the extent to which immigrants are employed, and there are some important variables. In the USA, but also in Europe, a particular feature of recent debates has been the argument that the character of international migration has changed. Family reunion means there is a larger proportion of economically inactive migrants. There are also increasing numbers of asylum-seekers who are not permitted to work legally for a certain period. More generally it has been suggested that new waves of migrants show less capacity to achieve social mobility and skill acquisition than earlier arrivals.

The overall employment rate of the foreign-born population in the EU is lower than that of the EU average. This rate varies significantly, however, according to place of origin. Immigrants from Western and Southern Europe have higher employment rates than the EU average, whereas those from other parts of the world have lower employment rates. Unemployment is particularly high among immigrants from Turkey, the Middle East, and Africa. There is also a strong gender difference. While foreign-born men have only a slightly lower employment rate than the EU average for men, foreign-born women have very significantly lower employment rates.

It is also important to note that local and city-level studies do not necessarily yield the same conclusions on immigrant employment and fiscal effects as national studies. At the local government level in a number of major European cities, for example, the net effect of immigrants on public sector budgets has been found to be negative, largely because of high levels of unemployment within certain immigrant communities. Ongoing research by William Clark in the nine main entry-point cities for new migrants in the USA demonstrates a fall in skills and income and increases in poverty and dependency relative to the native-born, a gap that has grown over time. Further analysis by Clark suggests that these problems are specifically associated with certain locales and certain ethnic and national groups. Unskilled Mexican migrants in Los Angeles County, for example, were found to be particularly impoverished.

It is important to conclude this section with one final observation. This is that there is often a gap between the findings of academic research such as that cited here, and public and even political opinions. Even where research points unambiguously to the conclusion that immigrants contribute to economic growth, do not compete for jobs, do not lower wages for the native-born, and represent good value in cost–benefit terms, this is not how they will necessarily be viewed. In the USA and Europe a correlation between negative public opinion on the scale of immigration and high unemployment levels has consistently been observed, even where no direct relationship between the two can be established. Similarly in Malaysia and South Africa, for example, immigration is regularly blamed for unemployment.

The second and third generations

Recently there has also been considerable attention paid to the economic performance of the children and even grandchildren of migrants—the second and third generations. Even though there are other factors such as political disenfranchisement and social and cultural isolation involved, their economic exclusion has been one of the most commonly cited reasons for recent unrest among the descendants of immigrants in various European countries.

Experts on this topic largely fall into one of two schools of thought. Optimists have suggested that, following the experience of European migrants to the USA, Canada, and Australia, while the migrant generation can be expected to experience some economic disadvantage, succeeding generations will come to compete on an equal footing. They cite many reasons why the first generation might fare badly in the labour market, including a lack of recognition for foreign qualifications, a lack of language fluency, and a lack of experience in the destination labour market. These reasons should not, it is argued, apply with the same force to the second generation. In contrast, pessimists suggest that this historical experience may not apply to recent migration, particularly where it originates from developing countries and involves visible minorities who will continue to experience discrimination.

Professor Anthony Heath, a sociologist at the University of Oxford, undertook with colleagues an extensive international comparative analysis on this topic, to identify the extent and causes of what they term the 'ethnic penalty'. Among other factors they compared unemployment levels between second and third generations of European and non-European ancestry in Australia, Canada, Israel, the USA, Austria, Belgium, France, Germany, the Netherlands, Sweden, the UK, South Africa, and Northern Ireland.

Their findings broadly confirm those of earlier studies. In all the study countries, the second generation of European ancestry basically experienced no ethnic penalty—in other words, their employment rates were the same or better than those of the native-born. Yet also across all countries, those of non-European ancestry did experience an ethnic penalty. This was particularly strong in Austria, Belgium, France, Germany, and the Netherlands. One factor accounting for variations between the study countries was the level of unemployment there—the ethnic penalty appeared to be highest where unemployment was highest.

In any such study it is difficult to explain the findings authoritatively as there are so many variables involved. Among the factors cited, however, were discrimination, widespread racism in some of the study countries, labour market flexibility, and human capital factors such as information, contacts, aspirations, and social identities. One of the overall conclusions of the study was that legacies from the past are not easily overcome, as evidenced in the findings by the experiences of African Americans in the USA and Catholics in Northern Ireland (although in the latter case the Protestants were the migrants).

One of the striking aspects of these and similar research findings is that the ethnic penalty for the second generation is experienced whatever the principles underlying integration policy. Thus second generations of non-European ancestry are basically as badly off in assimilationist France as in multicultural Britain. There is growing support for the idea that neither model necessarily works very well. Instead, it is argued that integration is best achieved through focusing on less abstract and more practical issues, especially language acquisition, training and education, labour market and economic incorporation, healthcare and other critical social services, and participation in civil and political life. It has been suggested that integration has worked in the USA more than in most other countries because of a hands-off approach by the federal government, which has fostered self-reliance and leadership among immigrant communities.

Migrants and politics

Across Western Europe, Muslim migrants and second and third generations are affected by disproportionate unemployment rates, which for many are compounded by education and housing problems. These underlying socio-economic tensions, it has been suggested, have been exacerbated in recent years by highly politicized identity issues related, for example, to the Rushdie affair in the UK, the 'war on terror', the invasions of Afghanistan and Iraq, and more recently the rise of ISIL. One outcome, according to Stephen Castles, Hein de Haas, and Mark Miller in *The Age of Migration*, is that: 'While the vast majority of Muslim immigrants eschewed fundamentalism, Western Europe certainly was affected by the upsurge in religious fervour that swept the Muslim world.'

A rise in fundamentalism, however, is just one aspect of a much wider literature concerned with the political impacts of immigration in host societies. Another intersection between immigration and politics has been the growth of anti-immigrant extremism. Anti-immigrant political movements have developed across most of Europe in the last decade; and have fared increasingly well. During the 2015 election in the UK, almost 4 million people voted for the UK Independence Party, which largely ran on an anti-immigration ticket. Current polls suggest that Marie Le Pen, the leader of France's Front National, will make it to the second-round presidential run-off in 2017, such is the popularity of her party's anti-immigration stand. In Denmark the Danish People's Party also won its biggest vote-share in its twenty-year history in 2015. In the USA, meanwhile, Donald Trump is championing the anti-immigration wing of the Republican Party. Some scholars have suggested, furthermore, that the emergence of right-wing parties has had anti-immigrant effects across the political spectrum. It has been argued, for example, that French socialist stands on immigration shifted to the right as support for the Front National increased. Whether or not this is an accurate analysis (other scholars refute it), it is clear that the success of such parties has been an important reason for the rise of immigration on political agendas across the industrialized world.

Besides fostering new parties and new issues, the academic literature identifies at least two other ways that immigration can impact on politics and political systems in destination countries. There is a vigorous debate, especially in Belgium, France, and the Netherlands, about political participation and representation for immigrants and their descendants where they are excluded from citizenship. During the 1970s and 1980s, they tended to mobilize outside the normal channels of political representation from which they were often excluded, for example, through involvement in industrial strikes, protest movements, hunger strikes, and urban riots.

In recent years an increasing number of European countries have granted certain political rights to immigrants, including that of voting and standing for office in local (but not national) elections. Largely this has been in response to a growing acknowledgement that the long-term residence of foreign nationals is a permanent phenomenon. Some argue that political participation in one's community of residence is a basic human right; it has also been suggested that excluding migrants from political participation can lead to social tension and conflict. In the countries of the EU, all EU citizens now have the right to stand for election as well as vote in local and European elections in their country of residence. A few countries (including Denmark, Finland, Ireland, the Netherlands, Norway, and Sweden) allow foreign residents from countries outside the EU to vote and run for office in local elections on the condition that they have resided there for a minimum period. In others (including Portugal, Spain, and the UK) local voting rights have been granted to certain nationalities on the basis of reciprocal agreements with selected countries.

Another potential impact on politics in the destination societies is through the formation of ethnic voting blocs among citizens of immigrant origins. Perhaps the best example is Soviet Jews in Israel, who comprise about 15 per cent of the Israeli electorate and have decisively affected the outcomes of every general election since 1992. Quebec's immigrant population voted against independence to influence the 1996 referendum on the future of Quebec in the Canadian Federation. In the tight 2002 German elections, the 350,000 Germans of Turkish origin also emerged as an important voting bloc. As a result of such potential impacts, political parties have increasingly appealed to the immigrant-origin electorate, for example, in the UK and USA.

The potential of the Latino voting bloc in certain states in the USA poses a particular dilemma for politicians. On the one hand, there is considerable political currency in taking a strong stand against irregular migration from Mexico. On the other hand, the Latino vote needs to be wooed. Excluding Puerto Ricans, some 42 million Latinos live in the USA—around 14 per cent of the population. The Latino vote can be critical in states such as California and Colorado. Furthermore, as one-third of Latinos in the USA are under the age of 18, their vote is likely to become even more important in the future.

Reducing the demographic deficit

A recent debate that has emerged is the extent to which immigration can help address the problems associated with the so-called demographic deficit: in an increasing number of industrialized countries the native population is simultaneously shrinking and getting older. Low birth rates have combined with increasing life expectancies and constant progress in healthcare. There are fewer young people and an increasing proportion of old people, many of whom are living for thirty or forty years after they have retired from work. In other words, there are fewer people who are economically active—working, sustaining economic growth, and paying taxes. Yet there are more people who no longer work but expect pensions and are increasingly dependent on the welfare state to pay for their medical and social care. In general the older they get the more care they require.

The demographic deficit is a particular problem in Europe, where the average European woman has just 1.4 children while it is estimated that to replace the current population she would need to give birth to 2.1 children. The population in Europe is shrinking as a result, as it is in China and Japan and will shortly begin to do so in the Russian Federation too. Indeed over 40 per cent of the world's population now lives in countries where the population is shrinking. At the same time there are important variations—some European countries, for example, are far less affected than others, and the USA has a growing native population, at least in part because of high immigration rates.

Most commentators agree that migration can be one way to begin to reduce the demographic deficit, although there is strong disagreement currently over how important a role it can play. As long as migrants are of a working age and able to find work, and as long as they work legally and therefore pay taxes, they can bolster the contribution of an otherwise diminishing working age population in the affected countries. It follows, some people argue, that more labour migration is in the economic self-interest of these countries. Without labour migration they will be unable to sustain current levels of pensions and welfare.

The counter-argument is that importing workers is only a short-term fix to ageing and shrinking workforces. This is because migrants of course also grow old themselves. What is more, there is evidence that even if they come from countries where there is a high birth rate, they often adapt their birth rates to the country in which they are working. So eventually migrants too will add to the cohorts of the elderly, without adequately replacing themselves with children to pay for their welfare.

The consensus appears to be that migration is not a 'silver bullet'—it cannot reduce the demographic deficit alone. It is, however, one important element in a suite of responses that will be required. Others include increasing incentives for women to have children (for example, through more generous maternity leave arrangements), raising the retirement age so that people work longer, increasing employment rates where there are significant levels of unemployment among the native population, and raising productivity through technological innovation. A less palatable alternative is to accept reduced pensions and other welfare benefits, or reduced levels of prosperity.

Enriching societies and cultures

Despite the obvious interdisciplinary nature of the topic of migration, there has been relatively little cross-fertilization between economic studies of immigration and other approaches. While it is difficult to put a price on non-economic impacts, they must nevertheless be factored into a balanced consideration of the overall impact of migrants in society.

The most striking way that migration has impacted on societies and cultures the world over is by making them more diverse and eclectic. Examples abound. Music styles as diverse as jazz, reggae, and *bhangra* originate in migration. Ben Okri and Salman Rushdie are world-renowned migrant authors, while the migrant experience has also stimulated a rich vein of post-colonial literature—Hanif Kureishi's *The Buddha of Suburbia*, Zadie Smith's *White Teeth*, Monica Ali's *Brick Lane*, and Chimamanda Ngozi Adichie's *Americanah* are all good examples. Albert Camus was a *pied noir*. It is often said that chicken tikka masala, an Indian dish, is now Britain's most popular meal. Spanish is now the most common language in certain districts of California and Florida. Around the world sports clubs have imported key players while national teams increasingly incorporate the descendants.

This effect has become even more intense as the diversity of immigration populations themselves has increased. The UK provides a good example. For well over a century the Irish have migrated to the UK in significant numbers, and they still are the largest foreign national group living there. After the 1950s there was significant immigration from former British colonies like India, Pakistan, Jamaica, and other Caribbean islands. Since 1970 immigration from Australia, Canada, New Zealand, and South Africa has been actively encouraged. In recent years this already diverse society has been further diversified by the arrival of peoples from still more countries. Since the 1990s, for example, there have been significant arrivals in the UK from Afghanistan, China, Iraq, Kosovo, and Somalia. Some people have described the situation in the UK today as 'hyper-diversity'.

At the same time, increasing diversity can present very difficult challenges. The headscarf controversy in France is a good example of how diversity can be difficult to accommodate with historical national principles. More practically, it is difficult enough, for example, to teach a class of thirty primary school children in, say, the UK or USA, where a handful speak Urdu at home. It is quite another challenge teaching a class where two children speak Urdu at home, three speak no English because they have recently arrived from Somalia, and two speak Mandarin as a first language. On the whole, however, societies that have managed to rise to the challenges of diversity have benefited incalculably.

The positive and negative impacts of diversity are most keenly felt in major cities, especially so-called 'global cities' like New York, London, and Hong Kong. Migration has become an integral part of the character of such cities in at least three ways. First, global cities in particular rely on highly skilled migration and ICTs to fuel the boom in international finance, legal services, and high-level business services such as accounting, advertising, and insurance upon which their economic status is largely based. Second, migrants often also fill the lower status jobs upon which all cities equally rely simply to function, for example, in transportation, waste disposal, hospitality, construction, and catering.

Third, and as a result of the availability of work, international migrants have become increasingly concentrated in global and other large cities around the world. Often they are concentrated in particular areas or districts as migrants tend to settle among their own community and close to places (such as churches, mosques, and community centres) that can give particular assistance that can be difficult to receive from local institutions. These concentrations of migrant communities add considerable colour and character to major cities around the world, forming world-famous districts like Chinatown and Little Italy in both New York and London. At the same time, migrants can be concentrated in the poorest parts of these cities, forming what are often referred to as ghettos.

Another way that migrants can be thought of as having enriched societies and cultures is through forging new transnational identities. Transnationalism is viewed by some as a political problem as it potentially undermines national allegiance. At the same time, it has potentially transformative social and cultural impacts according to Steve Vertovec, a leading theorist of transnationalism. He believes, first, that transnational migrants create new social formations that span borders. Second, that transnationalism is associated with a new form of consciousness, as increasing numbers of migrants have dual or multiple identifications. Third, that transnational migrants provide modes for cultural reproduction. They interpret and blend their cultures in new contexts to produce new, hybrid cultures. Fourth, that transnational migrants can be the focus for new avenues of capital. Fifth, that transnational migrants create new sites for political engagement. In particular, they can mobilize and influence politics in their home countries from abroad. Finally, it has been suggested that transnationalism results in the reconstruction of places and localities—in other words, that migrants can transform destination societies to be reminiscent of their own place of origin.

There are critics of the concept of transnationalism. Some say there is nothing particularly new about any of these processes. Others say they have been exaggerated and do not apply to most migrants in most parts of the world. Nevertheless, even the most ardent critics would probably agree that immigration has intersected with globalization to effect significant social and cultural, as well as economic, changes in destination societies. These changes are irreversible.

Chapter 8
The future of international migration

Since the first edition of this book, there have been some significant changes to the migration landscape that could not have been predicted. The Arab Spring, the Syrian conflict, the Ebola crisis, and the global financial crisis were all largely unexpected and have impacted patterns and processes of migration. While the growth in the number of migrants has remained relatively steady, the number of refugees has doubled. Few would have predicted the massive rise in remittances either. The evidence on the positive economic impact of migration has become stronger; yet anti-immigration politics and sentiments have increased. The rise in the number of migrants dying in transit has shocked many people.

Clearly trying to predict the future of international migration is a very unreliable exercise. Conceptual and data problems mean it can be hard to say just who migrants are and how many they are. Migration has become inextricably linked with a wider set of global economic and social changes, the dynamics of which can be subject to sudden changes. Migration and refugee regimes, which have important implications for the entry and subsequent status of migrants, can be affected by domestic political agendas that regularly change. Migration policies do not always have their intended effect. The implications of migration for subsequent second and third generations vary between countries and groups and cannot be modelled.

At the same time it is possible to discern current trends—in migration patterns and processes as well as policies—that it seems likely will contribute towards shaping international migration in the next few decades. Taking the main themes of each of the preceding chapters in turn, this final chapter identifies and briefly discusses some of these trends.

Asian migration

Most commentators would agree that the changing dimensions and dynamics identified in the first chapter of this book are likely to continue. International migration will probably continue to increase in scale and diversity for the foreseeable future and to affect every part of the globe, either directly or indirectly. The proportion of women among international migrants is likely to increase. Temporary and circular migration seems set to become an even more dominant norm. The potential for international migration to contribute to global economic growth will become greater, for example, as the scale of highly skilled migration grows; as will the social challenges of immigration as hyper-diversity becomes accentuated. In other words, migration will continue to matter.

Perhaps nowhere will it matter more in the foreseeable future than in Asia. In the 1970s and 1980s international migration from Asia grew dramatically. The main destinations were North America, Australia, and the Gulf States. In 2000 there were over 7 million Asian migrants in the USA—China was the second largest source of migrants each year after Mexico. OECD estimates put the Asian-born population in Australia at over 1 million, or a quarter of the total immigrant population and 5 per cent of the total population. There are at least 5 million Asian migrants working in the Gulf States, recently employed to prepare for the 2022 World Cup in Qatar.

Today, however, the main growth is in migration within Asia. Since the first edition of this book there has been an increase of almost 20 million migrants in Asia. According to the ILO, migration for employment within Asia has grown at around 6 per cent each year since 1995, despite the Asian financial crisis of 1997-9. The main sources are poorer countries with enormous labour surpluses, especially China and the Philippines, but also Bangladesh, India, Indonesia, Pakistan, and Sri Lanka. The principal destinations are the 'tiger' economies or newly industrializing countries (NICs) of East Asia, including Japan, Malaysia, Singapore, and Thailand.

The potential for further growth in international migration is enormous. There is no sign of a slowdown in economic growth in East and South-East Asia, and as a result these regions seem certain to pull in more migrant workers. China is now the second largest trader in the world and has overtaken Japan. This has happened in the space of just twenty years, and particularly in two regions—the Pearl River Delta (PRD) and the Yangtze Delta. The PRD is already running out of labour and has an estimated shortfall of 2 million workers. To compete with the Yangtze Delta region the PRD will have to look westwards for its workers, first to other Chinese provinces and then perhaps elsewhere in Asia and even to sub-Saharan Africa. The supply of labour within the region also appears set to grow as quickly as demand for it. The Indian subcontinent has a vast labour reservoir which shows increasing signs of moving. The Philippines and Indonesia also have significant population growth and both view labour export as a vital part of their economic strategies for the future.

What is also striking about Asian migration is its diversity. In many ways it encapsulates the changing dynamics discussed in Chapter 1. There is an increasing proportion of female migration, as many of the jobs for migrant labour in the region are in domestic work, entertainment, hospitality, and on clothing and electronics assembly-lines. There is also a growth in highly skilled migration and student migration in particular destined for North America, as well as at the other end of the spectrum significant populations of irregular migrants, refugees, and IDPs. Temporary migration remains the norm within the region, where the vast majority of labour migration is on a contract basis and because most Asian countries have resolutely resisted the notion of permanently settling migrants.

Internal migration

The purpose of Chapter 2 was to explain how conceptual challenges, data problems, and variations in state policies mean that defining a migrant is not always straightforward. Chapter 2—like the book as a whole—focuses exclusively on international migrants. Definitions become even more complex, however, where internal migrants are also included: there are far more of them yet few states count them; they move for just as wide a range of reasons; and sometimes they can be hard to distinguish from international migrants, for example, where borders shift, are unclear, or are porous.

It is estimated that in China alone there are 200 million internal migrants, compared with 232 million international migrants worldwide. What is more, internal migration appears set to grow at an even faster rate than international migration in the next few years. In the next twenty years a further 300 million Chinese are expected to migrate within their country—in other words, the number of internal migrants in China alone will more than double.

Its sheer scale alone makes the case for far more attention to be paid to internal migration than has been the case to date. The main reason, however, why internal migration matters for shaping the future of international migration is that it often precedes international migration. In other words, people who have moved from the countryside to the town or city often then continue to migrate out of the country. There are several explanations. One is that internal migration is self-selecting and comprises the more entrepreneurial within a society, and it is these people in turn who are likely to take the further risk of migrating across borders. In addition, they have experienced migration first-hand; and often have access to more education and information as a result of moving to cities, as well as to higher incomes and a wider choice of means of transportation. Internal migration can be particularly liberating for women, as cities are usually less conservative and patriarchal than rural areas, and provide the opportunity for women to become better educated and employed and more independent.

Internal migration can also contribute to development. It has been estimated that it has contributed up to 16 per cent annually to the growth of China's GDP in recent years. The main reason is that internal migration is one way of relieving unemployment in certain areas and filling labour market gaps in other areas. Limited research indicates that internal migrants also send home significant remittances. According to one estimate, the equivalent of over US$30 billion is sent home each year by Chinese internal migrants—mainly to rural areas by workers who have moved to the city. Their remittances have helped reduce the rural–urban income gap in China, decrease regional disparities in wealth, reduce rural poverty, pay for education and healthcare, and promote consumption and investment.

Climate change

Chapter 3 focused on the main drivers for international migration, and many of these can expect to be exacerbated in the coming years. Structural inequalities in the global economy will remain and continue to cause migration for the foreseeable future, which will be further facilitated by new revolutions in communications and transportation and the momentum of migration networks and the migration industry. Migration and globalization will continue to be inextricably linked.

One of the most vigorous current debates around migration— internal and international, voluntary and forced—concerns the potential impact of climate change and its effects. As often seems to be the case for migration, there has been a certain degree of hysteria, with predictions that drought and famine will drive millions of sub-Saharan Africans into Europe, or floods displace millions of Bangladeshis across the border to India.

In keeping with the overall tone of this book, there is a more reasoned approach. First, it is worth noting that there is still serious scepticism about whether or not climate change is occurring and if so whether it is anthropomorphic ('man-made') or part of a natural cycle of change. For me the evidence is clear that climate change is taking place, largely as a result of human activity. But what is far from clear is how its impacts will be felt, where, and when.

Second, it is important to understand that migration need not become an automatic response to the effects of climate change. A distinction is often made between 'slow onset' climate change effects like desertification or rising sea levels, and 'rapid onset' events like flooding. Migration is probably the last resort in response to the former—people can adapt agricultural methods, build sea defences, and so on. On the other hand where migration does occur as a result of such events, it is likely to be permanent, as homes and farms have disappeared permanently under water or sand. In contrast, migration is a much more likely and immediate reaction in response to rapid onset events, but is likely to be temporary—you should be able to return after the flood recedes.

Third, even where migration does take place in response to the effects of climate change, there is a variety of outcomes foreseeable. Some migration will be short term, some long term; some over a short distance, some over longer distances. The emerging consensus is that climate change is likely to drive more internal migration—from the coast inland, for example, and more internal displacement. Only a relatively small proportion of migration that will be attributable to climate change is likely to be across borders and between regions.

Such reservations notwithstanding, most commentators predict that a significant number of people will be displaced from their homes by the effects of climate change. There is very little evidence that this has occurred yet, and no consensus about how soon it will happen, where it will happen, and how many will be affected. But certainly looking to the future, climate change should be added to a list of potential drivers for migration and displacement.

Temporary migration

Chapter 4 focused on the ways that migration impacts on development in origin countries. The headline story will remain remittances, which according to all estimates will continue to grow even more. Diasporas are also likely to have a growing influence, as more and more origin countries realize their potential and reach out to mobilize them.

Return migration also seems set to increase, and as indicated in Chapter 4 probably represents the best long-term response to the challenges of the brain drain. One reason is that an increasing number of countries around the world are introducing temporary migration programmes, the point of which is to admit migrant workers for temporary periods of time, on the agreement that they will then return home. These apply both to high- and low-skilled workers.

In the early 1990s Germany was host to the largest number of temporary workers, and between a quarter and a third of a million have continued to enter each year. Today the largest number enters the USA—entries of temporary workers there have quadrupled since the early 1990s to over half a million annually. Of the industrialized countries, Japan now ranks third, with about

200,000 per year. Although the total numbers are significantly less, there have also been increases in the entry of temporary workers in other developed countries, especially across Europe, as new policies have been introduced to attract them.

An alternative way to gain temporary foreign labour is to regularize irregular migrants and grant them a legal work permit for a limited period. This was one of the driving forces behind Spain's regularization of about 700,000 irregular migrants in 2005, none of whom will be entitled to legal permanent residence. One of the immigration reform proposals introduced in the US Congress in 2005, the Cornyn–Kyl bill, would create a temporary worker programme that would be open to irregular migrants who first return home, but it too would not allow them to settle permanently in the USA. Malaysia, which attracts hundreds of thousands of workers, from Indonesia, Bangladesh, and the Philippines, is also attempting to turn its irregular migrant population into legal, temporary workers. The advantage of temporary migration for destination countries is that it can fill specific labour market gaps for a particular period and in a given location. It also avoids the long-term challenges of social integration, and as such reduces some of the negative attitudes and reactions of the host population towards immigration. For origin countries, temporary migration can reduce domestic unemployment and contribute to financial inflows through remittances. As migrants return after a set period the longer term impacts of the brain drain can be avoided, and furthermore there can be a brain gain as migrants return with additional skills.

There are two main reservations about temporary migration programmes. One is that they do not always safeguard the rights of the migrants. Concerns are regularly raised by human rights advocates, for example, about the treatment of contract domestic workers in the Gulf States. Even where direct exploitation is not a problem, some commentators believe that temporary migration will inevitably create two tiers of migrants—permanent migrants, who are entitled to full integration and its benefits, and temporary migrants, who are marginalized from mainstream society in order to ensure that they return.

The issue of return is the second subject of debate. Sceptics point to earlier experiences with temporary migration programmes in Europe, where 'guestworkers' who intended to stay for only short periods of time ended up settling permanently in countries like France, Belgium, and especially Germany. An old adage that is often used in this context is that 'There is nothing more permanent than a temporary migrant.' Another, that helps explain why, is a quote from Swiss novelist Max Frisch that 'We asked for workers and we got people.' In other words, once people earn a reasonable income, find a home, develop social networks—in short once people begin to 'feel at home'—they may not want to return when they are expected to.

From controlling to managing irregular migration

I hope Chapter 5 makes clear that irregular migration is a serious problem for all affected—although not always in the ways that media coverage and some politicians might emphasize. Efforts to stem irregular migration will continue to figure very high on migration policy agendas around the world. Yet there has been a subtle but significant shift in the language used by both policy-makers and academics in this regard in recent years. Whereas people once spoke of controlling irregular migration (and indeed international migration more generally), they now tend to speak of managing irregular migration.

The implication is certainly not that states are taking irregular migration any less seriously. It has been estimated, for example, that in 2014 alone the UK spent about US$5 billion trying to respond to the problem of irregular migration. There is, at the same time, a growing consensus that irregular migration cannot be stopped altogether. It will continue to be an important component of the future of international migration.

One reason is that the forces that determine the scale of international migration—including irregular migration—are powerful, for example, growing disparities in the level of prosperity and human security experienced by different societies. A second is that certain states lack the political will to address irregular migration. This applies in particular to states in certain countries of origin where irregular migration can be beneficial, relieving unemployment and providing a source of remittances and overseas investment. Even in destination states irregular migration can be viewed as quite functional from an economic perspective. As a result of deregulation, liberalization, and increasing flexibility, there is growing demand for various forms of unskilled and semi-skilled labour employed under precarious conditions. Irregular migrants provide a cheap source of labour and are often willing to work in sectors in which regular migrants and nationals are not.

A third reason is that policies aimed at reducing irregular migration have at times been ineffective and even had unintended consequences. Although the relationship is difficult to prove empirically, many academic experts think that one of the consequences of increasing restrictions on asylum-seekers in Europe, for example, has been to fuel the growth of migrant smuggling. Put simply, the argument is that people want to continue to enter Europe—for some because they are fleeing persecution and for others because they want to work—and if they cannot do so legally through applying for asylum they will do so illegally through employing a smuggler.

It has become clear that control measures such as border fences, biometric testing, and visas are, in isolation, unlikely to reduce irregular migration in the long term. They probably need to be combined with more proactive measures that address the causes of irregular migration, including achieving development targets to increase security and improve livelihoods in origin countries, as well as expanding opportunities to move legally. At the same time, it is unrealistic to expect states to dismantle controls altogether and open their borders, as is sometimes advocated. Most commentators now acknowledge that irregular migration will continue for the foreseeable future.

Reforming the international refugee regime

The international refugee regime is coming under increasing pressure. As demonstrated in Chapter 6, the number of refugees worldwide has reached a fifty-year high, and there is no obvious indication that the numbers will reduce any time soon. The proportion of refugees in a protracted situation, for whom there is no foreseeable durable solution, is increasing. Conditions for refugees around the world are probably deteriorating. The number of asylum-seekers has also reached a new peak; and the scale of asylum-seeking worldwide is compounded by the reality that an increasing proportion are found not to be legitimate refugees.

There is a funding crisis. Developed states are spending far more on their asylum systems—processing relatively small numbers of asylum seekers—than they contribute to UNHCR to protect and assist the vast majority of refugees in need.

The refugee definition is increasingly out of touch with reality. In particular, the 1951 Convention makes no reference to the environment. While the lack of clarity about the implication of climate change on displacement has been made clear, still there is little doubt that those who are displaced will be in need. At the moment there is no legal basis to protect them, and no international organization with the mandate or capacity to protect them.

In sum, the international refugee regime is placing unreasonable demands on states, and no longer protecting refugees. What is to be done?

As indicated in Chapter 6, there are good reasons not to try to renegotiate the 1951 Convention, however dated it may be. But it seems increasingly likely that the international refugee regime will need to be reformed. First, the international protection system needs to strive for accountability and impose sanctions on states that cause displacement, rather than focusing solely on the responsibilities of destination states. Second, it needs to reduce long-distance asylum-seeking. Methods might include strengthening protection of IDPs, processing asylum claims effectively in neighbouring countries, and making serious efforts to clamp down on smuggling. Third, the asylum burden on destination states should be relieved, by conceiving a fair system for burden sharing between these states.

Finally, serious attention needs to be paid to the current institutional arrangements for protecting and assisting refugees. UNHCR is increasingly working on populations like IDPs for whom it is not officially mandated. Other organizations like IOM are increasingly involved in working with asylum-seekers and refugees. The conceptual distinction between migrants and refugees is increasingly blurred, and discerning them in practice has become very challenging.

Respecting migrants

Chapter 7 introduced some of the main debates surrounding the economic, political, social, and cultural impacts of migration on host societies. Societies will, without any doubt, continue to struggle with the challenges of integration, as the scale and diversity of migration continue to increase, but also as they adjust to new global economic realities, a new security doctrine, and fundamental demographic changes.

Many commentators, however, fear that the rights of migrants risk being subsumed by wider national and international economic, political, and especially security concerns. Advocating for migrants' rights seems likely to be a very important component of the politics of migration for the foreseeable future.

While Chapter 7 provides examples of migrants who have broadly succeeded—ethnic entrepreneurs, the highly skilled, and transnationals—it also offers a reminder that certain migrant groups tend to be unemployed or fill low-status jobs, and live in poor conditions. There is substantial evidence that migrants can face specific disadvantages. They often have no or limited legal rights and suffer discrimination in the criminal justice system. They have limited access to education and healthcare. They are often excluded from civic participation. They can also suffer harassment and racial and religious hatred and violence.

Women face particular challenges. Of course some are highly successful, and migration can empower women. But women who migrate to marry, to become domestic labourers, or to work in the entertainment and sex industries are particularly vulnerable to exploitation and social isolation. The specific problems of trafficking have already been explained. Migrant women experience discrimination in the labour market in many countries. They can be subject to dismissal and even deportation if they become pregnant or become socially stigmatized if they contract HIV/AIDS. Migrant women can be at risk of violence from their spouse, especially in communities that are poor and marginalized. Furthermore, they are more likely than men to stay at home, making it more difficult for them to establish the language skills and social networks required to integrate in their new society.

Children also require specific attention. They are often more traumatized than adults by the fact that they have left behind a familiar way of life and find themselves in a society where the language and culture are quite different. Migration can lead to gender and generational tensions within households and these in turn can impact quite directly on the welfare of the youngest members. In the worst cases they can lead to violence and abusive treatment, particularly against girls and young women. As migrant children grow up, they can also experience a sense of alienation and uncertainties about their own identity and allegiances, especially if they encounter discrimination and xenophobia.

Towards a more rational debate

The overall aim of this *Very Short Introduction* has been to try to set the tone for a more rational debate about international migration. That debate should consider the evidence rather than rely on exaggerated media reports. It needs to place local concerns in a global context. It is important that it considers the totality of population movements rather than focus on just one or two groups, far less demonize them. It should use the word 'migrant' in a clear, consistent, and non-discriminatory manner. It needs to understand the limitations of statistics. A balanced view is required on the advantages and disadvantages of all aspects of migration, for all those affected.

Further reading

There is an enormous academic literature on international migration and refugees. A few key texts are identified here for further reading around the topics covered in each chapter of this book, but the list is by no means comprehensive. Much of the research that this book has drawn upon appears in journal articles: *Asia and Pacific Migration Journal* (Quezon City: Scalabrini Migration Center), *International Migration* (Washington, DC: Institute for the Study of International Migration), *International Migration Review* (New York: Center for Migration Studies), *Journal of Ethnic and Migration Studies* (Brighton: University of Sussex Centre for Migration Research), and *Journal of Refugee Studies* (Oxford: Refugee Studies Centre) are all important sources for up-to-date research articles. The website of the Centre for Migration, Policy, and Society (COMPAS) at Oxford University at www.compas.ox.ac.uk is also a useful starting point for further reading as is the Migration Information Source (www.migrationinformation.org) of the Migration Policy Institute. The websites of IOM (www.iom.int) and UNHCR (www.unhcr.ch) are good sources for reports and data on international migration and refugees respectively.

Chapter 1: Why migration matters

IOM, *World Migration 2013: Migrant Well-Being and Development* (IOM, 2013) is the most recent edition of a regular publication by IOM that provides an overview of contemporary migration issues and data.

Stephen Castles, Hein de Haas, and Mark Miller, *The Age of Migration: International Population Movements in the Modern*

World (5th edn, Macmillan, 2013) is the leading text on contemporary migration patterns and processes; and includes an overview of the main theoretical approaches and debates.

Robin Cohen, *The Cambridge Survey of World Migration* (Cambridge University Press, 1995) is a comprehensive collection of short articles on various migration issues worldwide over the past three centuries.

Chapter 2: Who is a migrant?

Alex Aleinikoff and Douglas Klusmeyer, *Citizenship Today: Global Perspectives and Practices* (Carnegie Endowment for International Peace, 2001) provides a global comparative overview of different models and policies for integration and citizenship.

Paul Boyle, Keith Halfacree, and Vaughan Robinson, *Exploring Contemporary Migration* (Longman, 1998) includes an overview of concepts and categories of international migration.

Global Commission on International Migration, *Migration in an Interconnected World* (GCIM, 2005).

R. Iredale, S. Hawksley, S. Castles (eds), *Migration in Asia-Pacific* (Edward Elgar, 2003).

Steven Vertovec and Robin Cohen, *Migration, Diasporas and Transnationalism* (Edward Elgar, 1999) is a collection of the key academic articles and chapters on diasporas and transnationalism over the preceding twenty years.

Chapter 3: Migration and globalization

Stephen Castles and Alastair Davidson, *Citizenship and Migration: Globalisation and the Politics of Belonging* (Macmillan, 2000) examines the impacts of globalization on new forms of migration and identity.

Stephen Castles, Hein de Haas, Mark Miller, *The Age of Migration: International Population Movements in the Modern World* (5th edn, Macmillan, 2013) is particularly strong on analysing the links between globalization and international migration.

Peter Stalker, *Workers without Frontiers: The Impact of Globalization on International Migration* (Lynne Rienner, 2000) adopts a global perspective to analyse trends and policies in labour migration and considers the debate on open borders for workers.

Chapter 4: Migration and development

Towards the 2013 High-Level Dialogue on International Migration and Development (UN, IOM, 2013) provides an up to date overview of recent research on the impacts of migration on development in both origin and destination countries.

Ron Skeldon, *Migration and Development: A Global Perspective* (Longman, 1997) provides an overview of the relationship between migration and development, with a particular focus on Asia.

UNDESA, *International Migration Report 2013* (UNDESA, 2013) focuses on contemporary international migration and contains data and in-depth analysis.

Chapter 5: Irregular migration

Ko-Lin Chin, *Smuggled Chinese: Clandestine Immigration to the United States* (Temple University Press, 1999) is an in-depth analysis of migrant smuggling between China and the USA.

Bill Jordan and Franck Duvell, *Irregular Migration: The Dilemmas of Transnational Mobility* (Edward Elgar, 2003) contains a theoretical overview of irregular migration, and a series of case studies of irregular migrant populations. Its focus is the UK.

David Kyle and Rey Koslowski, *Global Human Smuggling* (2nd edn, Johns Hopkins Press, 2011) is an edited collection of chapters on migrant smuggling and human trafficking around the world.

Chapter 6: Refugees and asylum-seekers

Barbara Harrell-Bond, *Imposing Aid* (Oxford: Oxford University Press, 1986).

Gil Loescher, *The UNHCR and World Politics: A Perilous Path* (Oxford University Press, 2001) describes the evolution of UNHCR and the international refugee regime.

Susan Forbes Martin, *Refugee Women* (2nd edn, Lexington Books, 2003) focuses on refugee women and policy recommendations.

UNHCR, *The State of the World's Refugees* (Oxford University Press, 2012) is the latest edition of a biennial UNHCR publication providing an overview of current asylum and refugee issues and data.

Chapter 7: Migrants in society

George Borjas, *Friends or Strangers: The Impact of Immigration on the US Economy* (Basic Books, 1990) analyses the economic impact of immigration in the USA during the 20th century.

Robin Cohen and Zig Layton-Henry, *The Politics of Migration* (Cheltenham: Edward Elgar, 1997) includes an overview of the political impacts of migrants and migration.

Alejandro Portes and Ruben Rumbaut, *Immigrant America: A Portrait* (3rd edn, University of California Press, 2006) analyses the various impacts of immigration in the USA.

Chapter 8: The future of international migration

Wayne Cornelius, Phil Martin, and Jim Hollifield, *Controlling Immigration: A Global Perspective* (2nd edn, Stanford University Press, 2003) compares policies on migration control and their underlying philosophies around the world.

Foresight, Migration and Global Environmental Change (London: Department for Business, Innovation and Skills, 2011) presents the best analysis and forecasts for the implications of climate change on migration and displacement.

Ari Zolberg and Peter Benda, *Global Migrants, Global Refugees: Problems and Solutions* (New York: Oxford University Press, 2001) is an edited volume of chapters on a variety of current and future migration and refugee challenges.

Index

SOCIAL MEDIA
Very Short Introduction

Join our community
www.oup.com/vsi

- Join us online at the official Very Short Introductions **Facebook** page.
- Access the thoughts and musings of our authors with our online **blog**.
- Sign up for our monthly **e-newsletter** to receive information on all new titles publishing that month.
- Browse the full range of Very Short Introductions online.
- Read **extracts** from the Introductions for free.
- If you are a teacher or lecturer you can order inspection copies quickly and simply via our website.

ONLINE CATALOGUE
A Very Short Introduction

Our online catalogue is designed to make it easy to find your ideal Very Short Introduction. View the entire collection by subject area, watch author videos, read sample chapters, and download reading guides.

http://global.oup.com/uk/academic/general/vsi_list/